S0-ATV-238

# The Dream

# *The Dream*

**4,000 Years of Theory and Practice**

*A Critical, Descriptive, and Encyclopedic Bibliography*

by

Nancy Parsifal-Charles

VOLUME TWO

LOCUST HILL PRESS
West Cornwall, CT
1986

LIBRARY OF CONGRESS CATALOGING-IN-PUBLICATION DATA

Parsifal-Charles, Nancy.
The dream.

Includes index.
1. Dreams—Abstracts. 2. Dreams—Bibliography.
I. Title.
BF1078.P33 1986 016.1546'3 86-15335
ISBN 0-933951-07-8 (set : alk. paper)
ISBN 0-933951-05-1 (lib. bdg. : v. 1 : alk. paper)
ISBN 0-933951-06-X (lib. bdg. : v. 2 : alk. paper)

Printed on acid-free, 250-year-life paper

Manufactured in the United States of America

DEDICATED

to

my father and mother

William and Nancy Charles

&

to my son

Cyrus

# Contents

## VOLUME ONE



## VOLUME TWO

**Lichtenberg (Georg Christoph). Lichtenberg Reader.** Selected Writings of Georg Christoph Lichtenberg. Translated, edited, and introduced by Franz H. Hautner and Henry Hatfield. 196p. Beacon. Boston, 1960.

There are few sources in English on the German physicist, mathematician, and writer of aphorisms, Georg Christoph Lichtenberg. As one of the earliest scientists to take an interest in the unconscious, Lichtenberg was preoccupied for a number of years with the meaning of his own dreams. He believed that dreams opened the doorway to self-knowledge. In fact, he wrote, in dreams "we often see ourself in a mirror, without thinking it is in a mirror."

Many of Lichtenberg's theories are not too distant from those later adopted by Freud and Jung. The theory that dreams may be but reflections of states prior to the development of individual awareness, suggests Carl Jung's idea of the collective unconscious.

Unfortunately, most of Lichtenberg's writings appeared only in local almanacs and specialized journals. So we must thank the editors for providing us with these fascinating passages of prose on dreams by this eighteenth century German whose theories reflect some of the more recent thinking on dreams, even though they were most probably considered absurd in his own time.

**Lincoln (Jackson Steward). The Dream in Primitive Cultures.** Introduction by C.G. Seligman. 359p. illus., notes, biblio., index. Cresset Press. London, 1935.

Pioneering study in cross-cultural analysis of dreams by an anthropologist who had training in psychology. This early book, Lincoln's Ph.D. thesis at the University of London, represents a cornerstone effort in the fusion of anthropology and psychoanalysis.

Lincoln was among the first to regard dreams as a transitional process between mental activity and cultural ends. He saw dreams as influencing many primitive cultures. The careful observer must consider the latent meaning of the dream before he can ever hope to fully fathom the true nature of the primitive culture he studies. These peoples live the dream much more so than we do in modern civilized societies: dreams brought on sacrifices, determined the nature of charms and totems, offered spiritual guidance, explained cures for illness, and prophesied the future.

On the other hand, Lincoln found no evidence that dream symbols were mentally inherited or formed, other than through the individual's own experiences. His view that his research cancelled all need of the racial memory postulate, certainly runs counter to Jung's theory of the collective unconscious. Further, Lincoln concluded, "cultural images . . . not only disappear when a culture breaks down but vary with different cultures and stand or fall with them."

This is certainly a major work on dreams and is not only to be considered anthropologically. Based upon library and field research, Lincoln examines carefully the structure, theory, and influence of dreams in primitive cultures; dream symbols; the type and form of primitive dreams; and, the discovery of "nuclear complexes" in primitive cultures through an analysis of the dreams.

The final half of the book presents dreams and dream interpretations among the Indians of North America, particularly the Yuma, Mohave, Navajo, Ottawa, Crow, Blackfoot, Ojibway, and Kwakiutl. The book closes with an attempted correlation of regional dream variations.

This fifty year old study is perhaps one of the top dozen books ever produced on dreams and dreaming.

A major work by a major scholar who has introduced us to a new world of dream interpretation.

**Linde (Shirley M.) & Savary (Louis M.). The Sleep Book.** 223p. photographs. Harper & Row. N.Y., 1974.

An artful, illustrated potpourri combining photography, folklore, physical exercises, and quotations in an effort to introduce the reader to sleep and dreams. Some mention is made of recent research in dream states, but the twenty-six pages (mostly filled with illustrations) leave but scant space for any serious discussion of dreams.

**Lindskoog (Kathryn). The Gift of Dreams.** 189p. Harper & Row. N.Y., 1979.

Personalized, popular presentation with a Christian orientation.

**Loehrich (Rolf R.). Oneirics and Psychosomatics.** 157p. index. Compass Press. McHenry, Ill., 1953.

In this introduction to "a new theory of psychoanalysis," Dr. Loehrich reports on his studies of hundreds of dreams of each of his many patients, seeking to base his interpretations on the parallels between the language of the dream and the language of the organism. He has formulated this data into a system which, he claims, forms part of the Unified Science.

In his explanation, Dr. Loehrich presents us with a fusion of "wake-state and dream-state blended occurrences," in which man, in his wake-state, subject to waking experiences, may be, without being aware of it, simultaneously subject to dream experiences.

He supplies us with a number of dream examples drawn from his own clinical files.

I must confess here that I do not believe myself qualified to judge the theory of Dr. Loehrich. In fact I am not certain that I even understand it. Perhaps the cautious introduction by Dr. Werner Wolff to this book puts a more fitting judgment when he concludes, "Future investigations will fully evaluate Mr. Loehrich's contribution."

**Lorand (Sandor). Technique of Psychoanalytic Therapy.** 251p. biblio., index. International Universities Press. N.Y., 1946.

This is the best elucidation of Freudian dream analysis for the beginning psychoanalyst that I have read. Dr. Lorand, on the Faculty of the New York Psychoanalytic Institute, presents his material in a simple, logical, and concise manner, with a clarity seldom found in professional instructional handbooks.

The author begins with an examination of the art of reconstructing the latent meaning of the dream from the manifest content. He cautions that those with only limited experience in psychoanalysis are prone to interpret exclusively through the symbolism of the dream. Instead the analyst must adhere to the basic rule of using the patient's free associations to the manifest content, and taking care not to attempt to translate the dream solely on the basis of his own associations. Although many symbols have universal significance, others can only be understood through the patient's associations.

Since one can become skilled in the art of dream interpretation only through experience, the author cautions the beginning analyst against hasty and excessive use of this technique. Additionally, Dr.

Lorand warns that sometimes the patient will bring in extremely distorted dreams with few or no associations. This is particularly true in character neuroses. Thus, no matter how many attempts the psychoanalyst makes to unravel the manifest content, associations cannot be defined. At this juncture, the analyst must work with the language of symbolism, which will require some knowledge of anthropology, mythology, folklore, art, and literature. It may require time until the patient realizes that his dreams have meaning, and must be accepted as a product of his own mind. Consequently, one should be cautious about beginning dream interpretation early in analysis.

A good rule is to begin with dream interpretation only after the analyst understands the life and circumstances of the patient, especially the conflicts which occasioned his or her illness. A good starting point is to explain the origin and meaning of dreams through the mechanism of the daydream, which no patient refuses to recognize as his own production. The analyst should explain the role of the censor, which creates distortion in order to make the dream seem meaningless or absurd. Dr. Lorand explains that a patient will usually accept the interpretation of his underlying desires if emotions are displayed in the manifest dream content. If the manifest dream seems flat and unemotional, the analyst is "sure to find emotional charges in the latent dream content through the patient's associations."

The author continues with an explanation of the mechanism of condensation, secondary elaboration, and the role of the changing nature of the dream, from the significant first dream, through subsequent changes in the nature of the dream during the course of analysis. The author emphasizes the importance of being aware of the regressive tendencies of the dream, and warns against the tendency to press the patient for dreams, or of overemphasizing to the patient the importance of dreams. Dr. Lorand concludes with a caution against hasty interpretation and analysis of frightening dreams charged with explosive content which the patient may not be ready to accept. Dreams relating to deep, fundamental conflicts such as homosexual tendencies, incest wishes, or death wishes fall into this category.

Technique of Psychoanalytic Therapy is an excellent exposition of a pure Freudian approach to psychoanalytic practice. Psychoanalysts emphasizing transference and countertransference as a substitute for dream interpretation will profit from it, as well as those in related fields searching for a clear presentation of Freudian therapy techniques.

**Lowe (Walter J.). Mystery & The Unconscious. A Study in the Thought of Paul Ricoeur.** 184p. Scarecrow Press. Metuchen, N.J., 1977.

Heavy academic study, which includes an examination of Ricoeur's analysis of Freud's Interpretation of Dreams. Obscure, and recommended only for those interested in the theological aspects of Freud's work.

**Lowie (Robert H.). Essays in Anthropology. Presented to A.L. Kroeber.** 422p. University of California Press. Berkeley, 1936.

"Dreaming in Relation to Spirit Kindred and Sickness in Hawaii" by E.S. Craighill Handy (pp. 119-128) and "Ojibwa and Ottawa Puberty Dreams" by Paul Radin (pp. 233-264) represent the dream papers in this collection. The first article contains dreams, analysis, and commentary on the important role of dreaming in old Hawaiian native culture. Hawaiians distinguish dreaming in deep sleep (when the spirit sees "the doings of the night") from the swift vision of half sleep. They also distinguish between the premeditated dream (dream incubation), procured in consequence of thought, and the unpremeditated dream.

In the paper on the Ojibwa and Ottawa puberty dreams, Radin seeks to show various stages through which the fasting-dream pattern passed as the culture of these two tribes disintegrated and the dream lost its original purpose. This is a finding similar to that reported by both G. Kelchner and J.S. Lincoln, suggesting a cultural determinant of dreams. (See notations on their works in this bibliography.)

**Lowy (Samuel). Psychological and Biological Foundations of Dream-Interpretation.** 260p. notes, index. Kegan Paul, Trench. London, 1946.

Dreams to Lowy are designed primarily to serve the emotional needs of the dreamer, acting as a safety valve and releasing the tensions developed during the conscious state. In maintaining the balance of the psyche, past and present merge during the dream state, suggesting that dream interpretation may best be accomplished through an intuitive rather than an analytical process.

Lowy was a student of Wilhelm Stekel. He designed this book as a primer or "psychological introduction to the science of dreams." There are individual chapters on symbolism, transformation, free association, food dreams, experimental dreams, archaic and infantile traits, concluding with a review of Freudian dream theories. An important work by this largely unrecognized Czech neuropsychiatrist.

**Luce (Gay G.) & Segal (Julius). Sleep.** 335p. tables, biblio., index. Coward-McCann. N.Y., 1966.

Survey of laboratory sleep research in 1960s, partially financed by the Public Health Service. Two chapters on dreaming contain a brief history of REM sleep discoveries, the effects of LSD on REM sleep, and research efforts in dream interpretation. Reprinted by Arena Books in 1977.

**Macario (Maurice Martin Antoine). Du Sommeil, des rêves et du somnambulisme dans l'état de santé et de maladie.** 307p. index. Perisse Frères, Impr., Lyon/ Paris, 1857.

Pioneering early study by physician and director of l'Institut Hydrothérapique de Serin. Dr. Macario discusses the causes of dreams (which he attributes to hypnotic hallucinations), relates dreams to the day residue activities of the dreamer (though he naturally does not suggest this modern term), and discusses the differences in dreams due to physical condition, age, temperament, and the character of the dreamer.

There are chapters on physiological dreams (dreams of the senses, hallucinatory dreams, dreams of illusions, emotional, and intellectual dreams), on morbid dreams, and an interesting closing chapter on the differences between dreams and the waking state. This is an essentially 19th century physiological interpretation of dreams. Much of it, however, might well have been published within the last few years. Modern experimental research has validated many of Macario's postulations.

It is a shame there is no English translation of Dr. Macario's fine work. I fear this review does not do it full justice. The book was reprinted in 1978.

**McCaffrey (Phillip). Freud and Dora. The Artful Dream.**

192p. notes, biblio., index. Rutgers University Press. New Brunswick, N.J., 1984.

A study of Freud's so-called "failed case" of dream analysis, in which the patient abruptly terminated her treatment because Freud reputedly sought to reframe the second of her dreams to suit his own preconceived theories. Dr. McCaffrey, a professor of English, cites this case as "a classic example of the male analyst's dogmatic imposition of biases on a female patient."

In his own hypothesis, Dr. McCaffrey offers his own theories on the "failure of psychoanalysis" when applied to aesthetics. I must confess that the author is a bit obscure in his writing, and I found myself impatient to get at the meat of his argument, which seems always to have eluded me. I had better leave this tome to a mind more brilliant than my own.

**McCarroll (Tolbert). Exploring the Inner World. A Guidebook for Personal Growth and Renewal.** 222p. sketches. Julian Press. N.Y., 1974.

Guidelines for inner imagery, meditation, and spiritual growth written by the founder and director of the Humanist Institute in San Francisco. Among the paths of self-exploration recommended by McCarroll is the personal dream. The author describes dream theories, explains how one works with her or his dream, and provides us with examples of dreams and dream interpretation.

McCarroll writes that we should listen to our dreams, for they provide us with a spiritual message meant to guide us through life. The most useful dream theory, he writes, is that contained in the Jewish Talmud, which advises: "The dream is its own interpretation."

**McCartney (Fred Morton). A Comparative Study of Dreams of the Blind and of the Sighted, With Special Reference to Freud's Theory.** 82p. Perkins School for the Blind. Watertown, Mass., 1913.

A largely overlooked early attempt to test Freud's theories of dreams through an evaluation of detailed questionnaires responded to by 96 totally blind students attending schools for the blind throughout the world. The researcher compared these with a control group of sighted individuals, mostly students attending Indiana University. McCartney was himself blinded at seventeen months, and reports that he has long held an interest in dreams. Included is a very good Freudian analysis of several of his own dreams, taken from a dream diary containing a total of 177 dreams.

McCartney agreed that those blinded before the age of five did not have visual dreams, but his primary concern was to evaluate the impact of dreams on the daily life and problems of his blinded subjects. He concluded that the blind and the sighted do not differ significantly in the purpose of their dreams, and that this purpose, along with the manifest and latent content of the dreams of both blinded and sighted, validate Freud's theories.

**McCreery (Charles). Psychical Phenomena and the Physical World.** 138p. notes. [Proceedings, Institute of Psychophysical Research, Vol. IV] Hamish Hamilton. Oxford, 1973.

One of the better modern books to appear that discusses the various philosophical questions arising from parapsychological phenomena. Mr. McCreery's interest in dreams focuses on lucid dreaming, providing the reader not skilled in French with some informative translations from the writings of Hervey de Saint-Denys, followed by an analysis of the writings of Celia Green who seeks to validate out-of-body experiences.

None of this has been scientifically proven, and the book itself is dated in that it has not incorporated some of the new experimental work done on lucid dreaming. With the absence of funds, the Institute seems destined to continue rewriting old and well worked data, and appears to be involved in no new, scientifically oriented research. Such has been the fate of parapsychological organizations over the past few decades on both sides of the Atlantic, and it does not seem likely that this condition will change in the near future.

Thus Charles McCreery's book serves up a banquet of interesting food for thought and speculation, but little of scientifically grounded substance.

**McCurdy (John T.). Problems in Dynamic Psychology. A Critique of Psychoanalysis and Suggested Formulations.** 383p. index. Macmillan. N.Y., 1922.

A solid criticism of the limitations and inconsistencies to be found in Freudian formulations, authored by a psychiatrist and lecturer at the medical school at Cornell University. This critical evaluation is based upon eight years of study with Dr. August Hoch, who worked primarily with patients exhibiting manic depressive disorders.

Some twenty pages are devoted to dreams. Dr. McCurdy begins by contesting Freud's theory that sleep is a regressive process, proposing, for him, an equally valid hypothesis: that we sleep in order to dream. He also finds difficulty with both foreconscious and censorship as related to dreams. While the basic elements of dreams are unconscious, he writes, remembered dreams are "only distorted selections of an endless riot of hallucinations." In this context, the author finds little role for diagnostic dream interpretation, since "these hallucinated free associations are unfit for conscious entertainment."

Not all of Dr. McCurdy's commentary is negative. He suggests that the best new ideas in this area might better come from the anthropologist than the physician. In this respect, the author is proposing an approach practiced today in cross-cultural research. As for Carl Jung, the author dismisses him largely from his pages, commenting that "No attempt has been made to consider the theories of Jung because, quite frankly, I cannot understand them."

While this reviewer does not agree with much of what Dr. McCurdy says, it is sad that this eloquent voice seems to have been lost. He marshals an imposing array of cogent and stimulating arguments which should not be forgotten, particularly by those who remain skeptical on many points in Freudian theory.

**McCurdy (John T.). The Metamorphosis of Dreams.** Kegan, Paul. London, 1925.

Several sources have referred to this title, but I can find no listing for it in the National Union Catalogue. This is possibly a British edition of the previous title.

**McDonald (Phoebe). Dreams. Night Languagc of the Soul.** 232p. Mosaic Books. Baton Rouge, La., 1985.

Popular explanation of dreams by a California psychotherapist with thirty years of clinical practice and teaching. McDonald emphasizes the mechanisms of the unconscious, the importance of intuition in dream interpretation, and the significance of sexual and instinctual drives in contributing to dream content. There are two chapters on the symbolic meaning of birth and death, and another on the animal as a symbol in dreams. Included as well are sections on children's dreams, and the archetypal and guidance dream.

Dr. McDonald provides numerous dream examples taken from her own clinical experiences, and follows these with her own associations and interpretations. Obviously the author has not totally rejected Freud, although the orientation is largely Jungian. I do not hesitate to recommend Dreams to the lay reader, particularly those with an interest in just how a professional therapist interprets a variety of dreams.

**MacFarlane (A.W.). Dreaming.** 52p. Edinborough, 1891.

**McGlashan (Alan). Savage and Beautiful Country. The Secret Life of the Mind.** 245p. Hillstone, N.Y., 1967.

In his tour through the inner recesses of the mind, the author suggests that the dream and creative imagination might prove the most productive response possible to the man lost in the military, political, and social chaos of modern times.

**Mach (Ernst). Contributions to the Analysis of the Sensations.** 208p. index. Open Court. La Salle, Ill., 1890.

Originally published in 1886, this study by a German physicist sought to apply the principles of physical science to the new field of psychology. The work contains a very small section devoted to dreams (Part 6 of the chapter, "Time-Sensation"), in which Mach expounds an experience not unlike lucid dreaming. "I dreamed of a walk in the woods," remembers Mach. "Suddenly I noticed the defective perspective displacement of the trees, and by this recognized that I was dreaming." Mach is well known to those with an interest in the history of science. In this book he supplies us with a brief comment on a method of dreaming some today believe to have been discovered only recently.

**Mack (John E.). Nightmares and Human Conflict.** 258p. biblio., index. Little, Brown & Co. Boston, 1970.

Study of the cause of disturbing dreams, the relationship between nightmares and severe anxiety, and the relationship nightmares may have to both creativity and pathological states such as acute psychosis. There are special sections on the nightmare in children, including determinants, clinical illustrations and the role of the child's nightmare in psychoanalysis. The author traces many adult nightmares to childhood origins.

Dr. Mack finds that the principal difference between the nightmare and psychosis lies in the fact that the effects of the nightmare are much more easily reversible in terms of the ability to reestablish reality or contact. The author does not totally agree that the nightmare is a dream that has failed, suggesting that this static interpretation does not take into account the task set before the mind of the sleeping individual, suggesting that the nightmare does not exist to preserve sleep but "is linked with a phylogenetically older mechanism that functions to preserve the organism itself."

Dr. Mack closes this interesting book with his theory of nightmares, in which he concludes that the nightmare may not only be made up of memories and other aspects of mental functioning that originated in early childhood, but may be linked with neurophysiological mechanisms that serve the functions of self-preservation and survival.

**MacKenzie (Norman). Dreams and Dreaming.** 351p. illus., index. Vanguard Press. N.Y., 1965.

Well-illustrated history of dreams and dream theory by a teacher of sociology at the University of Sussex in England. The author presents a clear exposition of the concepts of both Freud and Jung that is helpful for both the student and layman. His careful analysis of the trends in modern sleep research is naturally a bit dated.

The book ends with verbatim transcripts (including dream descriptions) of interviews with two female subjects after being given LSD. One subject reported more dreams, and more vivid images in dreams. She believed the greater clarity and color of the butterflies in a "very powerful dream," resulted from LSD. The second subject reported the LSD presented "realities," in the waking state far more vivid and lasting than those in the dream state. She indicated that she did not dream about the same images experienced during waking periods after taking LSD. Altogether, this is a compact, well written introductory text to the field of dreaming.

**McLeester (Dick). Welcome to the Magic Theater. A Handbook for Exploring Dreams.** 123p. illus. Food For Thought Press. Amherst, Mass., 1976.

A delightful potpourri of ideas, theories, and miscellaneous writings on dreams. Interspersed throughout are many fascinating sketches and drawings relating to the dream in all its aspects. Here one can touch on dreams in creativity, learning, and as a conscious fantasy, as spiritual or therapeutic tyranny, and as reflected in other times and other cultures. Mr. McLeester has thoughtfully provided the reader with an annotated dream bibliography. This little book can provide several hours of fascinating reading, which is more than enough to recommend The Magic Theater to all who love dreams for their own sake.

**McLeod (Stuart R.). Dreams, A Portrait of the Psyche.** 192p. index, mimeo. Century 21 Publishing. Saratoga, Calif., 1981.

The raw material presented consists of 145 dreams recorded daily by a woman over a ten week period. There is no interreaction between the dreamer and the Jungian author who subjects these dreams to the "tenets of Jungian dream analysis."

**Macnish (Robert). The Philosophy of Sleep.** 296p. D. Appleton & Co. N.Y., 1884.

This book might have contributed greatly to the science of dreams except for a fatal mistake made by the author. Dr. Robert Macnish, a Scottish physician, tied his theories to the phrenological concepts formulated by the German anatomist and physiologist, Franz Joseph Gall. Dr. Gall is remembered today as one of the first to ascribe cerebral functions to different areas of the brain, but he is less respected for his creation of the pseudo-science of phrenology. The author, however, devotes little attention to cranial configurations, relying instead on Gall's postulate: that the brain is the material apparatus by which the mind manifests itself. Following this naturalistic approach, Dr. Macnish argues that dreams are nothing but manifestations of the mind, and a product of the activity of the brain.

Once past this premise, however, one discovers in this author's writings much of value as relates to dream theory. Dr. Macnish was greatly interested in the "annihilation of time" during the dream, as well as the "absence of surprise" in the dreamer, no matter how startling the dream. While he argued that we could not identify all causes of dreams, a careful investigation might suggest their origin. He propounds that "Whatever has much interested us during the day, is apt to resolve itself into a dream." But he does not expand on that theory to include problem-solving.

On other pages, the author suggests a pre-Freudian idea of wish fulfillment. While dreaming, "even objects altogether unattainable are placed within our reach: we achieve impossibilities, and triumph with ease over the invincible laws of nature." Individuals, he notes, dream of what they do not have or are not. Hence the miser dreams of more wealth, while the choleric man dreams of passion. Macnish also conducted a thorough research of the early literature, indicating the relationship between dreams and both mental and physical illness, as well as the role of various sense stimuli on dream content.

Although The Philosophy of Sleep was widely translated and reprinted many times, it suffered by being characterized as but another questionable work on phrenology. With the scientific repudiation of that theory in the late 19th century, the work of Dr. Robert Macnish passed into near oblivion. It has not been cited by Freud, Adler, or Jung, none of whom possibly even consulted its pages.

**Macrobius (Ambrosius Theodosius). Commentary on the Dream of Scipio.** Translated with an introduction and notes by William Harris Stahl. 278p. Facsimiles, notes, biblio., index. Columbia Univ. Press. N.Y., 1952.

Macrobius' detailed commentary on the dream of Scipio is of interest to scholars more as a source of medieval science and precursor of the scholastic movement than as a primer on the dream. Nevertheless, he adopted Artemidorus' classification of dreams into five types: the enigmatic, prophetic, oracular, nightmare, and apparition or fantasy type dream. Macrobius states that the nightmare and apparition "are not worth interpreting since they have no prophetic significance." "The purpose of the dream," he argues, "is to teach us that the souls of those who serve the state well are returned to the heavens after death and there enjoy everlasting blessedness."

The writings of this fourth century A.D. cosmographer and oneirologist had a great impact upon the writings of Chaucer and, indeed, the entire medieval intellectual world, particularly his works on dream interpretation. Thus I found this book all the more disappointing, since there are few scholarly writings on Macrobius, and no translations from the Latin of his manuscripts on oneirology.

**Madow (Leo) & Snow (L.H., editors). The Psychodynamic Implications of the Physiological Studies on Dreams.** 167p. tables, notes. Charles C. Thomas. Springfield, Ill., 1970.

First major attempt at reconciling the discoveries of REM research with the accepted tenets of Freudian dream theory. In 1892, a psychologist, George Trumbull Ladd, suggested that the dreamer's eyeballs moved while he was dreaming. Ladd's speculations remained untested until 1952, when a graduate student in physiology, Eugene Aserinsky, collaborated with Dr. Nathaniel Kleitman in a laboratory experiment on eye movement with sleeping subjects. Utilizing a polygraph, the two investigators found that of the twenty-seven subjects awakened during periods of rapid-eye-movements (REM), twenty recalled detailed dreams. Conversely, of the twenty-three awakened during non-REM periods, nineteen failed to recall any dream whatsoever.

Since these discoveries, hundreds of laboratory tests have been conducted, revealing much additional data on this fascinating aspect of dream physiology, particularly on dream stages, and in objectively investigating when and how people dream. This collection of six papers seeks to relate these findings to clinical practice.

In "The Varying Uses of the Dream in Clinical Psychiatry," Drs. Roy M. Whitman, Milton Kramer, Paul H. Ornstein, and Bill J. Baldridge describe the many uses of the dream in clinical practice. They describe the possible therapeutic role of dream analysis in the diagnosis or treatment of illnesses such as depression or schizophrenia, and in discovering the forces motivating behavior or causing symptoms. They point to the helpfulness of dreams in determining treatment, including the dreams of those in marital therapy and the dreams of children. This is a well written paper describing the potentials of utilizing the dream, yet without overlooking the difficulties.

In "The Pharmacology of Dreaming Sleep and its Psychiatric Implications," Dr. Ernest L. Hartmann describes the effects of drugs on dreaming sleep. While noting that human pharmacological studies are still at an early stage, he shows that most clinically used drugs reduce dream time in man, at least when first given. He hastens to add that effects are not limited to pharmacological agents, but that almost anything which disturbs the dreamer's sleep (including fever, alcohol, new sleep environment) will reduce dream time. Apparently dream time is the first affected in sleep loss. Psychotic patients are both sleep and dream deprived. Dr. Hartmann postulates that recent investigations "support the hypothesis that the buildup and metabolism of serotonin within the brain is essential in regulating the sleep-dream cycle." He concludes that there is an important role for a drug that produces good sleep without depressing dream time.

In "The Phenomenology of Dreaming," Frederick Snyder estimates that an individual at age seventy would have experienced about 150,000 dream dramas, most unremembered unless awakened from a REM condition. He investigates the nature of dreaming itself, its biological aspect, and concludes with an analysis of the contents of 635 REM reports from 250 subjects' nights in a sleep laboratory. He quotes from a paper by May Whiton Calkins, published in 1893, in which she wrote that almost all dreams from which conclusions have been drawn have been particularly striking or unusual dreams, and therefore not fairly representative of the "warp and woof of dream experience." Dr. Calkins also noted the essential congruity and continuity of the dream life with the waking life. In his paper, Dr. Synder "confirms the findings" through modern REM research of these nearly one hundred year old speculations.

"A Sleep Researcher's Odyssey: The Function and Clinical Significance of REM Sleep" by William Dement, Harry Cohen, James Ferguson, and Vincent Zarcone, points out two different mechanisms in REM sleep. One is related to the production of REM periods, and the other concerns the elaboration and regulation of dream phases for performing its vital biological role. Their REM deprivation studies utilized the cat and rat. When deprived of REM sleep, a natural restorative process usually occurs. Dr. Dement studied REM and its process in mental illness, where he found that REM deprivation of 9 out of 9 actively ill schizophrenics did not show the usual compensatory REM rebound found in animals and normal humans.

Dr. Charles Fisher in his paper, "Some Psychoanalytic Implications of Recent Research on Sleep and Dreaming," surveys the biological findings relating to the sleep-dream cycle over the last decade. He compares these with Freud's observations. Finding that "a considerable amount of recent work supports Freud's safety valve and drive discharge theory of the function of dreaming," he contends that "it is my considered opinion that no single theory is sufficiently all-encompassing to explain the function of REM sleep. Most of the theories so far advanced are entirely physiological and too narrow in their scope." Dr. Fisher argues that any theory of REM sleep is complete "only when it considers all stages of development at all levels of integration: molecular, biochemical, physiological, neurophysiological, and psychological."

The "Neurohumoral Basis of Sleep" contains a further elaboration of Dr. M. Jouvet's classic work with cats. Examining paradoxical sleep, which is equivalent to dreaming in humans, Dr. Jouvet seeks to postulate a theory of the mechanisms of sleep.

All the professionals contributing to this collection are to be congratulated. It is a surprise to discover so many stimulating ideas this carefully developed in so few pages.

**Maeder (Alphonse E.). The Dream Problem.** Authorized translation by Drs. Frank M. Hallock and Smith E.

Jelliffe. 43p. [Nervous and Mental Disease Monograph Series No. 22] Johnson Reprint Corp. N.Y., 1970.

This monograph, originally published in 1916, represents the early views of the dream as exemplified by the Zurich school, then represented largely by Jung, Riklin, Silberer, and even Adler. The author writes that what the Zurich school has accomplished "is a natural outcome of what Freud gave us."

This work is concerned primarily with the "preparing function" of the dream rather than the cathartic, principally the role of unconscious activity such as fantasies, play, and vision. Dr. Maeder utilizes the dreams of an eighteen year old youth of a good family suffering from numerous neurotic problems and relates his therapy to associations, the experience of therapy, the significance of manifest dream content, and the dream set in a psychic environment.

One of his principal diversions from Freudian theory concerns dream symbolism. Dr. Maeder suggests that while the sexual interpretation may be the first step, it is only that, since the dream must also be interpreted in light of the concept of "re-birth," as outlined in Carl Jung's "Transformations and Symbols of the Libido." In the final part of this monograph, the author argues the basic differences between Freud's Vienna and Jung's Zurich school.

**Maeterlinck (Maurice). The Life of Space.** Translated by Bernard Miall. 194p. biblio. Dodd, Mead. N.Y., 1928.

The fourth dimension as seen by this noted poet and mystic, with a discussion of space, time, God, and dreams. In his section on the cultivation of dreams, Maeterlinck reviews the oneiric phenomena, suggesting that the investigations of the Marquis Hervey de Saint-Denys may be more valuable than all other dream research, including that of Freud.

Maeterlinck also emphasizes the relations of dreams to the future, specifically in a review of Dunne's An Experiment With Time, in which that author relies almost exclusively on dream premonitions to support his thesis that time is an aspect of the fourth dimension. To Maeterlinck, the idea of prophetic dreams is one that should not be in dispute. He cites the research work done by the British Society for Psychical Research, and Thomas Flournoy's Espirits et Mediums in support of his arguments.

Maeterlinck introduces us to three of his own dreams, each containing elements of prophecy. He suggests that one can learn the techniques for developing one's own prophetic dreams and, while he does not suppose that the mission of dreams is to warn the dreamer of good or ill fortune awaiting one in the future, still it may be that dreams give warnings which can be exploited to the dreamer's advantage.

Quoting from his earlier book, The Unknown Guest, Maeterlinck closes with his idea of the "perfect, entire and unalterable presence of that which for us is not yet." He refers us to this concept: "A bottle which I see falling in my dream to-day, whereas it will not actually fall until three days later, reveals a mystery just as extraordinary and inexplicable, and of precisely the same nature, the same origin and the same dimension as the mystery comprised in the prediction of the fall of a great empire which will not collapse until three centuries have passed."

There is, perhaps, little contemporary experimental science to support the contentions of Maeterlinck, but there is more than enough intuitive support to suggest that rejection of these theories based solely upon our inability to measure them quantitatively, or in a controlled environment, should not be justification alone for their rejection.

**Mahoney (Maria F.). The Meaning in Dreams and Dreaming. The Jungian Viewpoint.** 256p. index. Citadel Press. Secaucus, N.J., 1966.

Nontechnical explanation of Jungian dream interpretation. This book is certainly one of the most easily read and concise presentations of Jungian dream concepts. Mahoney begins with a description of Jungian theories and terms, particularly archetypes and symbols, followed by an explanation of the shadow, projection, anima and animus. The work concludes with sections on reductive, reactive, prospective, somatic, telepathic, and archetypal dreams. Recommended for those desirous of a lucid exposition of Jungian dream complexities.

**Malcolm (Norman). Dreaming.** 128p. biblio., index. Routledge. London, 1959.

Philosophical discussion of dreaming in which the author, best known for his study of Ludwig Wittgenstein, suggests that dreams are conscious experiences which are enjoyed during sleep. With this thesis, Malcolm argues against the dream theories of Descartes and Bertrand Russell. There are interesting sections in this book concerning the idea of dreaming as an exception, the temporal location of dreams, the continuity between dreams and waking life, and how one knows whether he is dreaming or awake.

Here is food for theoretical thought by one of the leading philosophers concerned with dreaming. Dr. Malcolm's writings, however, may be somewhat obtuse fare for those interested only in the practical applications of dreamwork.

**Malinowski (Bronislaw). Sex and Repression in Savage Society.** 251p. notes, index. World. N.Y., 1927.

This celebrated study is considered by many to be a pioneering work in the area of cross-cultural investigation. Dr. Malinowski reports here on his field investigations among the Trobriand Islanders in the Pacific, and gives a detailed and often exciting report on the habits and culture of these peoples. The Trobriand peoples live in a matrilineal society in which the newborn infant becomes a member of the mother's rather than the father's clan. The father plays a passive role in the family constellation and is not given any credit for a role in pregnancy. The Trobriands believed that the infant child was inserted into the mother's womb by a dead female relative.

Dr. Malinowski's work was one of the first to examine a primitive culture as a method of testing the theories of Sigmund Freud. Malinowski found great difficulty with these concepts, particularly the Oedipus complex, which he argued played no role in any matriarchal society. In addition, according to Malinowski, sex was prohibited in neither word, thought, nor action. In fact there existed no such thing as a repression of sexual desires among these peoples. Indeed, Trobriand children had complete freedom of sexual expression in talk and games, and in the selection of different mates.

Freudians considered this attack on Freudian theories so important that Dr. Ernest Jones, later Freud's biographer, wrote a defense of Freud's Oedipus concept. Jones argued that hatred of the father was clear in Trobriand culture in the obvious denial of the father's role in procreation. Later, Geza Roheim also defended the Freudian position, writing that Trobrianders had Oedipal legends in their mythology. Other writers, such as Victor Barnouw, have observed that Malinowski had no extensive background in psychiatry, administered no formal psychological tests, nor did he conduct any in depth interviews. Barnouw concludes that Malinowski's interpretation of Trobriand society, while valuable and important, may well be too simplistic.

All this relates directly to Malinowski's views on the role of the dream in Trobriand culture. Malinowski wrote that these people were not really involved with dreams. There was little evidence of spontaneous discussion of dreams, and he found no evidence of any system of symbolic dream interpretation. He does, however, discuss free fantasies and folklore among the Trobriand, and does comment on specific erotic dreams (see pp. 88-97). I know of no later study of these peoples in an effort to confirm or deny Malinowski's findings.

**Mallory (Herbert S., editor). Artistry and Dreams.** 319p. biblio. Univ. of Chicago Press. Chicago, 1929.

A promising title and disappointing book, with only one of the fourteen papers on dreams. In his chapter, "Artistry and Dream," Herbert Mallory begins with the "truism" that the dream process underlies all art. But the corollary concept that artistry is nothing more than a dream working its way through to artistic expression, he finds, is more suspect.

Professor Mallory investigates comments by leading literary figures on the role played by dreams and daydreaming in their writings, comparing these with Freudian theories of wish fulfillment. He finds the entire process wanting. True, there is some role in "self-regardant art," particularly the daydream. But, overall, he concludes that there is no concrete evidence to support the contention that true literary creation is but a dream form brought into a concrete mode.

**Mambert (W.A.) & Foster (B. Frank). A Trip Into Your Unconscious.** Foreword by Thelma Hunt. 379p. index. Acropolis Books. Washington, D.C., 1973.

Professional writer and layman uses Jungian dream concepts as a method of reaching one's unconscious. There is an explanation of common types of dreams, a discussion of the archetypal dream, instructions on keeping a dream diary, and a glossary of dream symbols. Nontechnical and readable.

**Mankowitz (Ann). Change of Life. A Psychological Study of Dreams and the Menopause.** 123p. notes, illus., biblio., index. Inner City Books. Toronto, 1984.

Jungian analyst's account of a menopausal patient's three years of therapy experiences. The analyst utilized the patient's dreams as an access to her unconscious during the critical period of menopause, and provides us with numerous dreams and their significance. She includes dreams which demonstrate fear of knowing, narcissistic mortification, sexual, death of the womb, anger, and three Jungian "big dreams": the archetypal masculine in women, the integration of the feminine, and, separation and transformation.

Mankowitz demonstrates how menopause, when accepted as a rite of passage, can transform a time of fear and anger into one of healing and self-renewal. This is an important book, not only for the analyst, but for all women approaching, and fearing, the "death of the womb."

**Mannlingen (M. Joh. Chr.). Auserlesenster kuriositäten merk-würdiger Traum-Tempel nebst seinem denck-würdigen Neben-Zimmern von allerhand sonderbaren Träumen.** [The Dream Temple and Its Remarkable Adjoining Chambers; About Strange Dreams of All Kinds] Frankfurt u. Leipzig, 1714.

Condemnation of dreambooks, for "if dreams are divine, then their interpretation would not be man's province, but only God's." Despite this, Mannlingen then proceeds, according to a review by Jolande Jacobi, to supply the reader with over 500 pages of dreams and dream interpretations, including warning and healing dreams, as well as dreams of treasure and dreams of death.

**Marais (Marie du). La Clef de tous vos rêves.** 143p. illustrations, biblio. Pic Ed. Ed. P.I.C. Bruxelles, Belgium, 1967.

Dictionary of dream symbols, with many beautiful illustrations from 17th century engravings. Ms. Marais has apparently consulted sources on dream symbolism as diverse as Artemidorus and Freud, Aristotle and Jung. Still this work remains a popular source of scant value.

**Marcus Aurelius Antoninus. The Communications With Himself of Marcus Aurelius Antoninus, Emperor of Rome, Together With His Speeches and Sayings.** A revised text and translation into English by C.R. Haines. notes, index. Harvard University Press. Cambridge, 1953.

This Roman emperor and Stoic is best remembered for his meditations, a form of self-analysis mixed with philosophy that is considered one of the great books of all times. In spite of his very strong Christian beliefs, Marcus Aurelius believed in dreams, a belief that was to leave him open to much criticism during his lifetime.

Marcus Aurelius argued that dreams could be viewed as God's helpers and for good fortune. In one discourse, Marcus wrote that dreams had given him antidotes against spitting blood and vertigo. Interestingly, Marcus himself was elevated to a godlike status following his death, and became known widely as a "dream-giver."

**Marcus (Irwin M., editor). Currents in Psychoanalysis.** 393p. notes, biblios., index. International Universities Press. N.Y., 1971.

The five contributions on dreams are excellent. William C. Thompson's "Overview" reviews recent studies, finding that they will require refinements and changes in psychoanalytic theory, particularly REM research. He notes the cycle of penile erection coincident with dreaming, and the occurrence of bed-wetting apart from dreaming. While such research tells the analyst very little he did not already know, "... the new biology of dreaming ... will profoundly influence future development of both theoretical and clinical aspects of psychoanalysis."

Dr. Jay T. Shurley's "Changing Concepts of Dreaming," reports that the young science of psychophysiology, while still in a state of confusion, holds great promise. "Experimental and Neurophysiological Investigation in Relation to Dream Theory" by Douglas Noble, argues that REM studies have confirmed Freud's original ideas, including his theory that a majority of dreams have a sexual aspect, particularly in "sustained penile erections and in the motor, especially oral activity of the neonatal period." Problem solving in dreams, on the other hand, "would appear to be a greater one than Freud had believed." He suggests some modification to the theory of the function of the dream as guardian of sleep.

Dr. Herbert F. Waldhorn's "Dreams, Technique, and Insight" discusses new therapeutic and technical considerations, while Dr. Melitta Sperling's analysis of the significance of children's dreams and sleep points out the importance of pregenital phases and preoedipal relationships in the genesis of sleep disturbances in children, especially during the anal phase of development and conflicts. The analyst may find that these types of sleep characteristics may be indicative of serious pathological disturbances.

**Marcus (Kate). On Initial Dreams.** 22p. The Analytical Psychology Club of Los Angeles. Los Angeles, 1954.

Analyst's discussion of the dream experienced either before or soon after the beginning of professional analysis. Dr. Marcus examines a series of initial dreams drawn from her own clinical practice, indicating a "new beginning," sometimes an "entrance through a narrow gate," and at other times, a transition, or coming to a frontier or bridge. She speaks of some dreamers who undergo a mandalalike movement, and includes symbols typical of initial dreams, such as water, the child-motif, or the plant-child. Dr. Marcus suggests that the analysand's initial dream is a significant touchstone upon which the analyst builds her or his interpretation in later therapy sessions.

**Marcus (Kate). The Stranger in Women's Dreams.** 15p. Analytical Psychology Club of Los Angeles. Los Angeles, 1956.

The female analysand's dream of a stranger or strange man should be viewed by the analyst as a dream symbol of urgency and meaning. Dr. Marcus describes clinical cases to underline her argument that the dream symbol of the stranger often indicates a temporary standstill in the area of the process of psychic integration. Once the analysand and analyst find where the "spiritual energy is blocked or is draining off into unproductive channels," a transforming renewal may be undertaken.

**Marcus (Kate). Separation Dreams.** 14p. The Analytical Psychology Club of Los Angeles. Los Angeles, 1960.

In the imagery and action of a separation dream, the dreamer experiences removal from another person, an impersonal object, or life situation. In women, separation dreams involve the husband being drafted into the military service or sent to a distant land where she cannot follow. Both men and women may dream of serious illness, death, or of destruction by fire, flood, or earthquake.

The author provides examples of separation dreams to argue that the separation of conscious from unconscious is a stage in the process of personality integration, and not an end in itself. Without separation, the two psychic systems cannot effectively relate one to the other. Separation dreams then may be viewed as a subtle indication of emerging independence from unconscious identification.

**Margolin (Malcolm, editor). The Way We Lived. California Indian Reminiscences, Stories and Songs.** 209p. notes. Heyday Books. Berkeley, Calif., 1981.

This collection contains one section in which four dream cult songs of the Wintu Indians are translated.

Beginning in the 1870s, a series of messianic movements swept the California Indians. The dream songs reflect this. A cult dreamer would meet a dead friend or relative in a dream, and receive a song. The song served as the focal point of a local dream dance cult, and, according to Margolin, helped invigorate native shamanism. Another section provides shaman dreams of the Mohave Indians, and dream experiences of the Luisño, Achumawi, and Yuma Indians.

**Maritain (Jacques). The Dream of Descartes Together with Some Other Essays.** Translated by Mabelle L. Andison. 220p. notes. Philosophical Press. N.Y., 1944.

Scholarly study of René Descartes and Cartesian theory. The book begins with an analysis of Descartes' three famous dreams of November 1619, purportedly setting him on his course that would ultimately lead to his role as the father of modern philosophy.

Descartes dreamed first that a tempestuous wind was whirling him about in the street. He struggles, hardly able to keep on his feet, seeking to reach the church of the College of La Fleche to say his prayers. At that very instant, he turns to show courtesy to a man he had neglected to greet, but the wind blows him violently against the church. Soon someone in the middle of the college courtyard tells Descartes that an acquaintance of his has a melon to give him. He experiences pain upon awakening, turns over on his right side, then prays to God for protection against the evil effects of this dream. Falling asleep once again, he dreams of an event that "fills him with terror." He awakens to a burst of noise like a crack of lightning, and sees thousands of sparks in his room. In a third dream, Descartes sees upon a table a dictionary and a Corpus poetarum, or collection of significant poetry. It is open to a passage by Ausonius,

"What path shall I follow in life?" Then an unknown man hands him a bit of verse. The "Est et Non" of Pythagoras catches his eye.

Descartes reports in his journal that he decided while still dreaming to interpret these dreams. The twenty-four year old soldier/philosopher took the first two dreams as a warning about his past, and the final dream as a revelation bearing upon his future. Afterwards Descartes wrote that his dreams instructed him to search for knowledge within himself.

The author gives us a semantic rather than a psychological interpretation of the dreams of Descartes, though he does debunk those writers who have suggested that this dream revealed to Descartes the idea of a universal science that would link all possible human knowledge together into an all-embracing wisdom.

There is no discussion of the rich symbolism evident in these dreams. The Church of La Fleche, for example, was the location of the Royal College, where Descartes studied for ten years under the Jesuits. Shortly before these dreams, he became a Rosicrucian, possibly pointing to his unsettling dream experiences at the church.

Their significance for philosophy and scientific methodology, however, is not in what the dreams of Descartes really meant, but in what he believed they meant. His interpretation of those dreams provided motivation enough to alter his life, and begin the serious inquiries which evolved into the great Cartesian contributions to science and philosophy.

**Martin (E.M.). Dreams in War Time. A Faithful Record.** 63p. The Shakespeare Head Press. Stratford-Upon-Avon, 1920.

This is one of those nostalgic "slim little volumes"

which seems to appear during great wars, particularly the first great war. In this mixture of dreams remembered and poetry created, Mr. Martin recounts in a psychic sense a classic case of what Dr. Freud would have considered wish fulfillment. The dreams remembered treat not the horrors of battle, but the forests and squirrels and castles of home in rural England. A beautifully written fragment from an author noted for his writings of the fields and streams in England's west country.

**Martin (Lawrence T.). Somniale Danielis.** An Edition of a Medieval Latin Dream Interpretation Handbook. 212p. notes, bibliography. P.D. Lang. Frankfurt a Main, 1981.

In his informative introduction, Dr. Martin examines the various manuscript codices of the Dream Dictionary of Daniel the Prophet, the celebrated interpreter of Nebuchadnezzar's dreams. This work seems to have been one of the most popular and widely copied by scribes during the Middle Ages, from the ninth century on, and has been found in most centers of learning (both religious and royal libraries).

The Latin texts of the Middle Ages appear to have been translated from a Greek text of the seventh century. Copying by hand by many scribes and through many different editions resulted in a number of errors (termed pollutions) resulting in such errors as the original Dreams of Aves (Birds) being transcribed as Dreams of Apes. Once begun in a major manuscript, such pollutions were carried on indefinitely. As for the manuscript proper, only Latin scholars need consult this very erudite tome, for Dr. Martin supplies us with various versions of Daniel's dream dictionary in that language only.

Many commonplace or chapbook dream dictionaries of the seventeenth through the nineteenth centuries seem to have been based largely upon one form or another of the original dream dictionaries of Daniel and Artemidorus. Dr. Martin concludes that most of these, because of loose translations and errors, are largely of little value to us today.

**Martin (P.W.). Experiment in Depth. A Study of the Work of Jung, Eliot and Toynbee.** 275p. notes, index, Pantheon. N.Y., 1955.

This exploration of myth and symbols in the writings of the psychiatrist, poet, and historian (all giants in their respective fields) is a risky venture into a new dimension of cross-discipline analysis. Unfortunately, as concerns the extensive mention of dreams and dream analysis in this book, it fails to measure up to the reader's anticipation. Martin can never seem to escape the magic grip of Jung, and both Eliot and Toynbee suffer proportionately.

**Masserman (Jules H., editor). Violence and War.** With Clinical Studies. 284p. notes, index. Grune & Stratton. N.Y., 1963.

With three papers on dreams: "An Investigation of Parental Recognition of Children's Dreams. A Preliminary Report" by Irving Markowitz, Joseph C. Mark and Stanley Seiderman; "The Significance of the Emotional Experiencing of Dreams in Psychoanalytic Therapy" by Frederick A. Weis; and, "Report on Dreams in a Lifetime Struggle with Conscience" by John A.P. Millet.

The children's study, based upon dream picture identification, tended to show that parents are more responsive to their own child's dreams than to the dreams of other children. The paper on emotion as experienced in dreams, emphasizes the patient's full subjective acceptance of his dream as a reflection of his personality.

In the final paper, Dr. Millet supplies a series of dreams experienced by a man in his early sixties who withdrew from a career in the priesthood just prior to seminary graduation in the face of deep-seated religious doubts coupled with severe emotional disturbances. The author finds that the dreams of this patient illustrate "vividly the difference between the obsessional conflicts of a patient who has no conscious concern with religious beliefs and practices and those of a manifestly devout man whose lifetime of struggle with his conscience represented a wish to escape from the tyranny . . . of a need to believe certain dogmas."

**Masserman (Jules H., editor). Development and Research.** 296p. notes, index. Grune & Stratton. N.Y., 1964.

Research studies include "Experimental Dream Studies" by William C. Dement and "The Role of Dreams in Psychoanalysis" by Walter Bonime. In the first, Dement reviews the recent literature in REM studies, concluding that experimental studies of dreaming as revealed through REM research "indicate that its importance lies more in its nature as an organismic state rather than a psychological experience." The discussion by Drs. Allan Rechtschaffen, Harmon S. Ephron, Patricia Carrington, Montague Ullman and Irving Bieber amplify, and in some points disagree with, Dement's conclusions. The second study by Walter Bonime suggests that the dream serves not only as a potential source of illumination of the form and function of the patient's personality, but also as a continuing challenge to the analyst to risk cooperative intimacy with the patient.

**Masserman (Jules H., editor). Adolescence, Dreams and Training.** 205p. notes. Science & Psychoanalysis. Vol. IX. Grune & Stratton. N.Y., 1966.

The section on dreams, which has nothing to do with adolescents, devotes a scant nineteen pages to four papers, and to an introduction by Montague Ullman. All were presentations given at the panel discussion of the Annual Meeting of the Academy of Psychoanalysis in May 1965.

William Offenkrantz suggests two hypotheses on the psychological organization of a night's dreams worked through at the University of Chicago Sleep Laboratory. These validated, he writes, Freud's theories concerning the patient's defensive/adaptive waking behavior and the sequence of ego functions in the dreams of the night.

Helen B. Lewis discusses pre-sleep experience and dreams as related to an experimental approach to dream content and dream recall. Her report is based on an experiment involving the introduction of an emotionally charged event just before a person goes to sleep, then retrieving the subsequent dream content.

Dr. Walter Bonime's paper laments the tendency of the analyst to pay lip service to dream content, then disregard the dream data in psychotherapy when other phenomena appear "intuitively to have more immediate significance."

Harley C. Shands' paper suggests that "dreaming represents a kind of proto-artistic experience." In his "Dreams as Drama," Dr. Shands reports that to some extent the dreamer is always a *voyeur* rather than a participant in the dream, although each dream is actually a drama played out in terms of important interpersonal relationships. He concludes with the observation that both Freud and Piaget appear to have anticipated modern physiological findings. The dreaming process is experienced again as a playback of other experiences, as in a drama. "The dream is thus in a sense pure play without consequence."

**Masserman (Jules H., editor). Dream Dynamics.** 194p. bibliography. [Science and Psychoanalysis, Vol. XIX] Grune & Stratton. N.Y., 1971.

A collection of twenty papers by various contributors, many suggesting revisions and, in some cases, outright refutation of Freudian dream theory and interpretative techniques. One of the most radical criticisms is given by Walter Bonime, who rejects Freud's contention that dream interpretation is the "royal road to the unconscious," suggesting instead that dream interpretation "is primarily a device by which the analyst trains the patient to structure personal data to conform to the therapist's personal and theoretical beliefs."

Roger Bastide's excellent paper on dreams and culture points out that the dream "takes place at the crossroads of nature and culture, because it arises both from the physiology of the nervous system and from the culture from which its images and meaning one gives them derives." Bastide belicves that the dream should take into account all possible liaisons between nature and culture. Conversely, he suggests that here both Freudian and Adlerian psychoanalysis fail, since they do not offer "definitive solutions but products of our civilization." He suggests that a global theory would "provide access to the various mechanisms by which nature acts in various cultures to produce human phenomena."

The question of the nature and function of sleep fantasy in the child is given definition in a series of longitudinal studies of dreams in children undertaken by David Foulkes, and, the results of a workshop showing differing responses by various psychoanalysts to traditional dream theory and interpretation is also dealt with in a spirited, if inconclusive, series of discussions.

Very little of this book is likely to warm the psyches of traditional Freudians. One reviewer, in fact, was so negative as to wonder "why they are not equally emboldened to change the name of the discipline under which they operate." Yet the papers as a whole, and particularly the post-paper critiques, stimulate, even though they do not entirely satisfy.

Those seeking a new, unified theory of dreams and their interpretation will not find it in Dr. Masserman's collection, but they will encounter a number of disturbing, if unsettled, questions.

**Masters (Brian). Dreams About H.M. The Queen and Other Members of the Royal Family.** 144p. index. Blond & Briggs. London, 1972.

This is a very unfortunate title for a delightful book on the history and nature of dreams. The author, a professional writer, gives us a witty, fascinating account of bizarre and absurd dreams, dreams of prophecy, and dreams of vivid imagination. I would heartily recommend Mr. Masters' book to those interested in dreams of historical characters as well as for those little bits and pieces of historical dreamlore which have always intrigued me.

**Masterton (Graham). Women's Erotic Dreams.** 235p. Warner Books. N.Y., 1976.

Lurid rather than informative work. Disappointing fare from this otherwise conscientious writer. I would recommend his later book on this topic.

**Masterton (Graham). 1,001 Erotic Dreams Interpreted.** 302p. Warner Books. N.Y., 1977.

More serious effort than the title would indicate. The author, a professional writer, has done his research, detailing the contributions of the best modern dream-workers on this topic. There are chapters on twenty common erotic dreams, how to keep a dream diary, ten erotic dreams interpreted, and an explanation of the therapeutic aspects of erotic dreaming. A one hundred and ten page erotic dream thesaurus is well written, which shows the author's serious rather than tantalizing intent.

**Mattoon (Mary Ann). Understanding Dreams.** 248p. notes, biblio., index. Spring Publications. Dallas, 1984.

Dr. Mattoon collected all Jung's thoughts and writings on dreams and their analysis scattered throughout the twenty volume Bollingen Series, along with references to dreams found in his letters and speeches. This book is a modified version of the author's doctoral dissertation, which contained 972 separate entries. In addition, Dr. Mattoon provides a number of interesting dream examples taken from her own clinical practice, and gives a most satisfactory nontechnical exposition.

Besides offering an accurate record of Jung's approach to the dream, Understanding Dreams makes a valuable reference source. An appendix contains nineteen dreams analyzed by Jung. Includes a helpful bibliography and index. An earlier edition appeared under the title, Applied Dream Analysis, in 1978.

**Maury (Louis Ferdinand Alfred). Le Sommeil et les rêves. Etudes psychologiques sur ces phénomènes et les divers états qui s'y rattachment.** Troisième Edition, revue et considerablement augmentée. 484p. notes. Librarie Académique. Paris, 1865.

A pioneering effort in dream theory and analysis by the celebrated 19th century French physician who specialized in mental disorders. This work represents the culmination of Dr. Maury's work on hypnagogic hallucinations and his important observations on the relationship between the dream and mental disturbances.

Maury investigated the role of suggestion in dreams, post-dream recollections, and the intervention of instinct in determining emotions during dreams. He was one of the first physicians to attempt to develop a methodology for the use of dream interpretation in therapy. Dr. Maury's work had considerable influence on Sigmund Freud. His writings are quoted extensively in Freud's own The Interpretation of Dreams and, though somewhat dated today, much in this book is still of interest. Modern dream theory owes much to the earlier efforts of this French medical investigator and Greek scholar.

**Meddis (Ray). The Sleep Instinct.** 148p. tables. biblio., index. Routledge & Kegan Paul. London, 1977.

The author proposes the theory that sleep serves no important function and that modern man can live happily without it. This theory is also held by Bernie Webb (see Sleep, the Gentle Tyrant). Meddis finds that recent research supports the contention that dream-deprivation does not harm anyone; contrarily, that some procedures for treating depression actually involve depriving patients of their dreams (either by drugs or waking patients during REM periods).

**Megary (R.L.). An Investigation into the Mystery and History of Dreams.** 2 volumes. [American Institute for Psychological Research] Albuquerque, N.M., 1985.

This book, as far as I can ascertain, has been published, even though I can locate it nowhere in any university library. Perhaps the publisher's price ($127.25) is responsible for the limited dissemination. A request for information about the book has gone unanswered.

**Megroz (Rodolphe Louis). The Dream World, A Survey of the History and Mystery of Dreams.** 318p. notes, index. Dutton. N.Y., 1939.

Essentially a compilation of short passages on the nature of dreams, and the recounting of significant dreams by noted authorities and celebrities. Emphasis is on the dream as an instrument of creative inspiration in the work of poets and artists, and the parapsychological aspects of dreaming. There are excerpts on physical disorders as a cause of dreaming, dreams of the dead, recurring, vivid, and flying dreams, creative dreaming, dreams of ghosts and symbols, telepathy in dreams, and dreams of the future. Much of this may be found in The World of Dreams and The New World of Dreams, although the student of the role of the dream in the arts may find here citations not found in similar compilations.

**Meier (Carl Alfred). Ancient Incubation and Modern Psychotherapy.** Translated by Monica Curtis. 152p. notes, biblio., index. Northwestern University Press. Evanston, 1967.

Invaluable historical account of dream incubation in ancient Greece, with its emphasis on healing and promoting good health. Includes studies of Asclepius, Serapis, incubation at the Oracle of Trophonius, and the incubation ritual in the Asclepian sanctuaries. Published originally in German by the Jung Institute in Zurich in 1949 (with an introduction by Carl Jung), this book is not for Jungian scholars alone, but should be a point of departure for all interested in the use of the dream in healing.

**Meier (Carl Alfred). Jung's Analytical Psychology and Religion.** 81p. Southern Illinois University Press. Carbondale, Ill., 1977.

Only one of the four papers included concerns the interpretation of dreams. This paper was originally a lecture given by Dr. Meier while teaching at the Andover Newton Theological School.

The paper is primarily an historical exposition of the development of Jung's theory of dreams, including the influence of the work of Herbert Silberer in Vienna. Dr. Meier discusses Jung's views that the dream has a dramatic structure that can be looked upon as "inner dramas," which may be analyzed as one would a stage play. As a continuation of this concept, Jungian theory holds that a dream is a whole, with both beginning and ending, conflict, and solution.

Stage drama, in fact, most probably had its true origins in dreams. To narrow the dramatic concept even further, it is argued that the dream is more like a mystery drama or therapeutic myth, in which the solution is there for the analyst to discover.

There is much more in this twenty-two page exposition of Jungian dream theory, its origins and principal concepts. Many Jungian writers are pedantic and obscure; Meier is not. I would highly recommend it to all who wish a clear and stimulating discussion of the topic.

**Meier (Carl Alfred). Der Traum als Medizin: Antike Inkubation und Moderne Psychotherapie.** 200p. notes, biblio. Daimon Verlag. Zürich, 1985.

New, revised edition of the previous title, available as of this writing only in German. In this work Meier adds commentary on his efforts in utilizing Greek dream incubation therapy techniques successfully while giving psychotherapy to psychotic patients previously regarded as medically incurable. A valuable contribution to the study of how ancient dream practices influence modern psychotherapeutic practice.

**Meltzer (Donald). Dream Life. A Re-Examination of the Psychoanalytic Theory and Technique.** 184p. notes. Clunic Press. London, 1984.

One of the best works in recent years which seeks to expand on original Freudian dream concepts and make them applicable to the practicing psychoanalyst of today.

In his early pages, Dr. Meltzer examines Freudian dream theory, suggesting that Freud did a grave injustice to the dream by identifying it as the guardian of sleep. Failure in Freud's neurophysiological thinking, the author argues, led him incorrectly to establish a topographical model based on those mechanisms that made possible disguised wish fulfillment, i.e., the censor, condensation, symbolism, and displacement. Meltzer writes that Freud would have been better served to reconsider his theory after he had formulated his initial structural model.

In the middle portion of the book, Dr. Meltzer proposes a revised dream theory in which dreams are considered not only as wish fulfillment mechanisms, but as vehicles for both thought and the rudiments of thought. In the final third of the book, the author discusses the practice of dream investigation, using clinical examples through an informative psychoanalytic process. He presents the patient's dream, follows with his observations on the dream and his role in that dream process, and concludes with a personalized reaction, pointing out his contribution to the interplay.

A most rewarding, if sometimes complex, report on the employment of personal interaction in psychoanalytic therapy. For those who believe that Freud's excessive interest in association weakened his dream theories, this book should be required reading.

**Meseguer (Pedro). The Secret of Dreams.** 232p. Newman. Westminster, England, 1960.

The position of the Catholic Church on dreams and dreaming, containing a history of the church's views and current evaluations.

**Messer (William S.). The Dream in Homer and Greek Tragedy.** 102p. notes. bibliography. Columbia University Press. N.Y., 1918.

The author examines the dream as an originating cause or directing principle of the action in the poem or play, a moving force in the evolution of narrative or plot, and in the introduction of smaller incidents and episodes.

A detailed exposition is given to The Iliad and The Odyssey of Homer, where Dr. Messer finds scant use of the dream in the former, but extensive use of the dream device in the latter. Messer continues with his analysis in the plays of Aeschylus, Sophocles, and Euripides.

In the discussion of the works of Aeschylus (the first dramatist to utilize dreams successfully), Messer cites Greek sources on the rites of purification after evil dreams (p. 62), with comments throughout the monograph on early Greek dream interpretation, in some cases comparing Greek dramatic symbolization with the writings of Artemidorus. He provides us with a bibliographic note on ancient dream incubation.

**Meunier (Paul) & Masselon (René). Les Rêves et leur interprétation.** 211p. Blound et Cie. Paris, 1910.

The authors are two French psychiatrists, whose work consists of their own clinical observations as well as a review of current French literature on the role of the dream in therapy. Significantly, the authors take no note of the work of Freud, although they do suggest the value of dream interpretation in psychiatric therapy.

Drs. Meunier and Masselon discuss the distinguishing features of dreams in neurosis and insanity, the latter revealed in "an obsessive or impulsive tendency," predating such evidence in a waking state. They suggest that the psychiatrist investigate the nature of the patient's dream as an indication both of the nature of the illness, as well as a further indication of progress in therapy. Interpretation of dream symbols is discussed on a rather sweeping basis. Dreams of blood or red, for example, appear as recurrent dreams in premenstrual periods, as well as in patients with heart disease and in dreams of those who suffer from epilepsy.

**Michals (Duane). Sleep and Dream.** 64p. illus. Lustrum Press. N.Y., 1984.

Poetry and photographs combine to evoke the author's inner world. More a personal psychic statement than dream book.

**Miller (Gustavus). 10,000 Dreams Interpreted.** 617p. Rand McNally. Chicago, 1979.

First published in 1931. One of the more frequently issued American dream chapbooks designed for the unsophisticated audience. It has appeared under different titles, one of the more recent being The Dictionary of Dreams: 10,000 Dreams Interpreted.

**Miller (Shane) & Cayce (Hugh Lynn). Dreams: The Language of the Unconscious.** 94p. A.R.E. Virginia Beach, Virginia, 1972.

Analysis of dreams based on the teachings of the noted psychic, Edgar Cayce. Strong religious orientation.

**Milner (Marion). The Hands of the Living God. An Account of a Psycho-Analytic Treatment.** 444p. glossary, bibliography, index. International Universities Press. N.Y., 1969.

Account of a psychoanalyst's twenty year treatment of a deeply schizoid woman. The detailed narrative contains both Freudian and Jungian experiences, and is particularly interesting for the inclusion of a number of dreams reported during therapy, accompanied by Dr. Milner's interpretations, and numerous dream pictures drawn by the patient.

**Mindell (Arnold). Dreambody: The Body's Role in Revealing the Self.** Edited by Sisa Sternback-Scott and Becky Goodman. Introduction by Marie-Louise von Franz. 219p. illus., notes, index. Sigo Press. Los Angeles, 1982.

Graduate degrees in physics and psychology make for excellent ingredients in this very fine Jungian potion whose central theme is that our bodily processes mirror our dream life. Understanding how the unconscious speaks through this language of the body can lead to greater psychological awareness. The author's researches cover a wide range of sources, from physics and medicine, to Eastern philosophy and shamanism.

Dr. Mindell makes a strong case for integrating the waking body with the dream in full adaptation of our cultural consciousness with our unconscious being. As expected, this professional Jungian therapist provides the reader with a full panorama of mythology and symbolism, but none of it couched in terms or pedantry which will break the flow of the book. Recommended for Jungian professionals and laymen alike.

**Mindell (Arnold). Working with the Dreaming Body.** 133p. index. Routledge & Kegan Paul. Boston, 1985.

Dr. Mindell continues his studies of the dreambody with an examination of the various potential techniques possible for using the dream to uncover the meaning behind physical disease. He has developed a system designed to uncover thc "exact mode or channel in which the person is moving," following a person's natural tendencies. The central idea is to employ this process to discover the inner undercurrents leading to or suggesting physical disease. As the author says, "To date, I have not come across one case in which a body symptom's process was not reflected in a dream, and I have seen many hundreds of physically ill people and many thousands of dreams."

The author approaches the diagnosis of illness via dream interpretation through a host of interesting discussions, including the role of the dreambody in a fairy tale, in evaluating interpersonal relationships, and in accommodating one's inner life to concerns of the external world. Mindell writes clearly and easily, interspersing his analytical passages with a rich body of dream examples drawn from clinical case studies.

Working with the Dreaming Body will profit all interested in the role of the dream as an inner mirror of the nature of external maladies. My only reservation is that the book, restricted to but 133 pages, is too slight to cover this important topic as fully as is required. Still we have here a significant contribution to the literature of dreams and bodily illness that can profit the layman and Jungian analyst alike. Much remains to be said, but Dr. Mindell's work has put us all several giant steps ahead along that path.

**Mitchell (Sir Arthur). About Dreaming, Laughing and Blushing.** 157p. W. Green & Sons. Edinburgh, 1905.

**Monteith (Mary E.). A Book of True Dreams.** 220p. index. Heath Cranton. London, 1929.

Parapsychological aspects of dreamwork reported upon, including van Eeden's theory of the "dream body," the use of telepathy in influencing dreams, cases of prophetic dreams, occult dream symbolism, dreaming of the dead, and dream intelligence.

Ms. Monteith has made extensive use of the files of the Society for Psychical Research, adding to these the fruits of her own researches into memoirs and personal accounts, along with several personal interviews. None of this will add an ounce of proof or conviction to persuade the skeptical. There is certainly no pretext at scientific methodology here, so we have another contribution to the occult dream genre which those already convinced will delight in, and those not so persuaded would do better to ignore.

**Moon (Sheila). Dreams of a Woman. An Analyst's Inner Journey.** 207p. illus. Sigo Press. Boston, 1983.

Personal autobiography of a Jungian analyst, illustrated with the author's own dream experiences. The narrative and dreams cover a period of roughly fifty years, and include dreams about Carl Jung and other celebrated Jungians, as well as personal dreams relating to Dr. Moon's own search for individuation. Two hundred thirty-five dreams are printed in italics, followed by Dr. Moon's interpretation of each.

Moon was both a student and close friend of Emma Jung, Gerhard Adler, Toni Wolff, and others of the Zurich school, and this autobiography reflects the influence of each in her 30 years of struggle against "a negative animus," with the accompanying years of psychic anguish and physical illness. This book makes a major contribution to Jungian studies, representing not only a remarkable and sensitive autobiography of one woman's struggle for self-discovery, but as an example of the potential value of dreamwork in that difficult quest.

**Moore (Thomas Verner). The Nature and Treatment of Mental Disorders.** 312p. notes, index, Grune & Stratton. N.Y., 1944.

Non-Freudian interpretation by a professor at the Catholic University of America, intended as a text in clinical psychiatry. In his discussion of the use of dreams in analysis, Dr. Moore rejects the Freudian theory of dreams, suggesting instead that the analyst consider those proposed by Adler and A.E. Maeder, who compared the dreamer to an artist seeking in his dreamwork the solution to his actual conflict. (See A.E. Maeder, The Dream Problem, Nervous and Mental Disease Monograph 22. 1916.)

**Moreau de Tours (Jacques Joseph). Du Hachisch et de l'aliénation mental.** 431p. notes. Fortin, Massin, et Cie. Paris, 1945.

A truly pioneering work by one of the first psychiatrists to suggest that mental symptoms are manifestations of the disturbances of the whole personality. Dr. Moreau (1804-1884) found dreams to be similar in structure to hallucinations since they are made up of the same materials as psychotic symptoms. Since dreams represent the transient psychopathology of the normal individual, they can also serve as a point of contact between the healthy and insane mind. Dr. Moreau suggests that the psychiatrist employ dreams as one technique for understanding psychosis, since the underlying basis of delirium and the dream are essentially the same.

Psychiatric historians, notably Drs. Franz Alexander and Sheldon Selesnick, have pointed out that Moreau's concept of the two modes of existence may actually have been the first written expression of the concept of the unconscious, even though the author did not use that term. As the title suggests, the author even experimented with hallucinogenic drugs in order to gain his own experience of the psychotic state.

This book is the reprint of the original edition. Surprisingly, this important contribution apparently escaped the otherwise careful attention of Sigmund Freud.

**Morris (Jill) The Dream Workbook.** 197p. notes, index. Little, Brown & Co. Boston, 1985.

A simple, well written explanation of the meaning and importance of dreams, followed by an exercise workbook designed to allow individuals to realize the full potential of their dreams. It may be a commentary on the present state of psychoanalysis and on the popularity of dreams that the author is a practicing psychoanalyst in New York who developed this workbook while conducting a dream workshop at Cooper Union.

Morris' explanation of orthodox dream theories ranges from Freud to Jung, and from the Gestalt School to an examination of Senoi techniques and the Iroquois Indian methods of acting out dreams.

While this summary is well presented, it touches briefly on important, and debatable, points and so demonstrates many of the weaknesses inherent in popularizations of this kind. Morris, for example, suggests that while Freud made many contributions, a number of his theories have since been proved wrong. She writes that modern research "has disproved Freud's belief in dreams as guardians of sleep . . . " [there are still noteworthy dissenters to this argument], and fails entirely to consider the long-standing psychoanalytic view that individuals are least capable of understanding their own dreams. That, in fact, is not only a core principle in the practice of psychoanalysis, but the justification that allows psychoanalysts to take our money.

If one can lay aside these concerns, it is possible to agree with the publisher that the author has produced a helpful guide designed to introduce the beginning dreamer into such techniques as lucid dreaming and dream incubation. None of the techniques are new. Rather, Dr. Morris has blended into her dream workbook some of the best, or at least most popular, techniques developed by the likes of Stephen LaBerge, Fritz Perls, Ann Faraday, Patricia Garfield, and Kilton Stewart.

Still The Dream Workbook is shackled with the heavy chains common to the genre of popular dream explanations and self-help guides that have appeared over the past few decades: many oversimplify, and most promise more than they can deliver. Sadly, many are written by professionals who should be aware that playing with dreams can be potentially dangerous, particularly for the emotionally unstable. Does such dream play alter messages the unconscious may be sending us? May it actually block messages from the unconscious? And if so, what does the unconscious do? Nothing? Or does it convey its message in other ways, even, perhaps, through physical or emotional illness? One may wonder as well whether long-term dream modification may present flash-back problems as experienced by certain users of LSD? And, finally, can one with training and long-term practice in dream modification effectively undergo dream therapy in psychotherapy?

I have no evidence that any of the problems suggested above actually exist. But I have no evidence that serious investigators have pursued these concerns with statistical or experimental research either. And this is what concerns me.

There exists no Food and Drug Administration to police the ideas and suggestions of popular writers on the dream, nor should there necessarily be such an organization. Yet I am troubled with the possibility that some modern professionals are producing nothing more than fallacious dream chapbooks that are not much different from those of centuries past, except in their free intermixing of sometimes unsubstantiated ideas and promises with valid experimental research.

Before his death, Calvin Hall mentioned this concern. He was uncertain, so I extend that concern here.

**Mosak (Harold H., editor). Alfred Adler: His Influence on Psychology Today.** 306p. notes. Noyes Press. Park Ridge, N.J., 1973.

If Freud's method of dream interpretation might be termed causative, seeing the dream as a clue to the past, then Adler's dream theories could be termed purposive, in that they point towards the future and the problems that lay ahead.

Dr. Joseph Meiers, in his paper discussing Adler's methods of utilizing dreams as an aid towards healing, provides us with a case study of dreams where early recollections were not really applicable, or at least not used, in the analyst's use of Adlerian "shortcuts" in therapeutic situations. Dr. Meiers had an opportunity to follow-up this case after ten years. During those years the patient's life-style showed most satisfactory progress as a result of Adlerian therapy.

The author gives us the case history of the patient, initial psychiatric evaluations, early treatment, dreams in the patient's past, methods of inducing attention to dreams, dreams occurring during the course of therapy, and the healthier life-style experienced by the patient following therapy.

An excellent single patient exposition demonstrating the use of Adlerian dream therapy techniques in treating sexual disfunction.

**Mosak (Harold H.) & Mosak (Birdie). A Bibliography for Adlerian Psychology.** 319p. indices. Wiley. N.Y., 1975.

Bibliography of the writings of Alfred and Alexandra

Adler, along with those of over one hundred other Adlerian proponents, sponsored by the Alfred Adler Institute of Chicago. There are almost 70 references made to writings on dreams and the use of dreams in the Adlerian approach to analysis. The sources are not annotated.

**Moses Necromantus. Mussulmanische Traumdeuter und Wahrsager, vollständigste Traumbuch mit auf die Erfahrung Aller Völker und Zeiten gegrundeter Auslegung aller Träume . . .** Leipzig, 1900.

A popular dream book containing almost 4,000 dream interpretations, reputedly given by Moses Necromantus, court dream interpreter to the Emperor of Ethiopia. I have been unable to locate a copy, but Jolande Jacobi has referred to it as a popularized version of an ancient Islamic dreambook.

**Moss (C. Scott). The Hypnotic Investigation of Dreams.** 290p. notes, bibliography, index. John Wiley & Sons. N.Y., 1967.

Still an important touchstone for all interested in hypnotically induced dreams. The first section of the book consists of Dr. Moss's introduction to the subject, covering early experiments, clinical experiences, and more recent experimental studies on dream hypnosis and advances in related areas. There follows a substantial number of selected readings relating to experimental methodology, the question of dream symbolization and interpretation, the effect of posthypnotically suggested dreams on the sleep cycle, and the vital question for psychotherapists: Is the night dream and the hypnotic dream the same, or is it different?

This last question is not answered conclusively within the covers of this book. In his paper, William Domhoff presents experimental evidence supporting the similarity of the two; Margaret Brenman, in another paper, even advances this proposition to argue that hypnosis is probably most clinically fruitful when contrasted with spontaneous dreams. On the other hand, the experimental research of Theodore X. Barber argues for the opposite conclusion.

This book presents an important summary of hypnotic dream research, augmented by a collection of significant papers on this topic. Unfortunately, more recent experimental evidence in the two decades following its publication has yet to appear in book form.

**Moss (C. Scott). Dreams, Images, and Fantasy: A Semantic Differential Casebook.** 302p. tables, biblio., index. University of Illinois Press. Urbana, 1970.

Clinical psychologist with twenty years' experience in hypnotherapy sums up his work and research. This work includes an analysis of the hypnotic investigation of symbols in dreams, accompanied by a clinical experiment conducted in the interpretation of dreams during hypnosis. The author admits that, though he has confidence in the use of hypnosis in dream analysis, the results of his own experiments were inconclusive. He recommends further research.

**Muensterberger (Warner) & Axelrad (Sidney, editors). Psychoanalysis and the Social Sciences. Vol. V.** 297p. notes. index. International Univ. Press. N.Y., 1958.

This collection of papers contains a study by Saul Rosenzweig on Josef Popper, whose book <u>Fantasies</u>

of a Realist, anticipated Freud's major dream theories, particularly in the areas of cultural awareness. The author provides translations from Popper's book to support his contention, and includes some interesting biographical data on Popper and his writings. Another paper, "On Some Psychological Factors in Pictorial Advertising," by Richard R. Sterba, relates key switch-words and pictorial representation to Freud's dream theories.

**Murchison (Carl, editor). A Handbook of Child Psychology.** 711p. notes, index. Clark University Press. Worcester, Mass., 1931.

Largely dated collection of papers on child psychology, redeemed in some measure for this reviewer by the careful study of children's dreams by Dr. C.W. Kimmins (pp. 527-554). Kimmins supplies us with a report on the dreams of normal children, some interesting experimental studies of children's dreams conducted in the 1920s in England (comparing the differences in dreams by age groups), and the results of research into the dreams of children in industrial schools, who were largely the product of "wrecked homes and dissolute parents."

Included as well are the results of studies made of the dreams of deaf and blind children, and an analysis of the child's own concept of his or her dream. The paper closes with an intriguing section on dream control, drawn largely from the writings of Arnold-Forster and De Sanctis. Included are a number of dream examples. The study ends with a bibliography.

**Murphy (Gardner). Challenge of Psychical Research. A Primer of Parapsychology.** 297p. notes, illus., index. Harper. N.Y., 1961.

This survey of parapsychology includes dreams of premonition (one involving a railway collision, another of a decapitated woman whose body was found 24 hours later), experiences in telepathic dreams, as well as dreams predicting death. Many of the sources cited are familiar, though in a few cases Murphy draws from examples in his own files.

**Murray (Edward J.). Sleep, Dreams and Arousal.** 407p. tables, index. Appleton-Century-Crofts. N.Y., 1965.

Textbook format in The Century Psychology Series, authored by professor at Syracuse University. One chapter on dreams and sleep introduces the reader to REM dreams, function of dreams, and physiological aspects of the dream state.

**Myers (Frederic W.H.). Human Personality and Its Survival of Bodily Death.** 2 Volumes. 700;660p. notes, index. Longmans, Green & Co., London, 1915.

The book is essentially a collection of reports drawn largely from the files of the British Society for Psychical Research, and, as such, does not stand the rigorous test of modern experimental control. The Society was founded in 1882 by physicist William Barrett, the Reverend Stainton Moses, the philosopher Henry Sidgwick, and classical scholar Frederic Myers, who would play the major role in the Society's first two decades.

Myers touches on dreams throughout, supplying reports of apparitions seen in dreams, dreams and hypnosis, the role of memory in dreams, prognostication in dreams, and dreams of famous people.

Myers believed that both sleep and dreams are important to waking life and that those thoughts and feelings lying just beyond the limits of man's consciousness are expressed through dreams. He discussed the "illusions hypnogogiques" and "hypnopompic illusions," those images that both precede and follow closely after sleep. He felt that these illusions are in fact products of the dream that provide the conscious mind with an intense visualization of the inner being at a moment when the dreamer is able to grasp its importance. Myers believed that the dream is a "supernormal" element expressing the wishes of the soul.

If Dr. Myers could prove even a small portion of the thesis suggested by the title, his book would undoubtedly be the most popular best-seller in the history of the printed book. But it is not, and Frederic Myers' weighty tome lies hidden today on the back shelves of musty libraries, unconsulted by all but the most rabid proponents of life after death.

**Myers (Frederic W.H.). The Subliminal Consciousness.** 593p. Arno. N.Y., 1976.

Collected writings of Myers, first published in Proceedings of the Society for Psychical Research. One article, "Hypermnesic Dreams," originally written in 1892, contains the author's exposition on dream precognition, dream transference, and other examples of the occult in dreams and dreaming. It is regrettable that Arno, a New York Times publishing company did not see fit to prepare this book with new and sequential pagination, preferring instead to simply photocopy the originals. Psychic dream researchers will find it exasperating as a research tool.

**The Mystic Dream Book. 2500 Dreams Explained.** 186p. Arco Publishing Co. N.Y., 1983.

Originally published in England in 1963. Another version of the same publisher's Dreams. Hidden Meanings and Secrets, except this dream dictionary seems to be a closer lineal descendant to the medieval dream chapbooks, which in turn may be traced to the likes of the dictionary of Artemidorus.

**Nagera (Humberto, et al.). Basic Psychoanalytic Concepts on the Theory of Dreams.** 121p. index. Basic Books. N.Y., 1969.

Research compendium designed to provide the reader with a clear exposition of Freud's dream theories, including heavily documented sections on the latent dream content, affects in dreams, dream fantasies, censorship and distortion in dreams, symbolism, wish fulfillment, day dreams and dream interpretation.

**Nand (Satya). The Objective Method of Dream Interpretation.** 251p. notes, biblio., index. Northern Indian Printing & Publishing Co. Lahore, 1944.

Indian psychoanalyst elaborates on his "objective method" of dream interpretation, explained largely through a detailed account of the manifest and latent nature of three dreams taken from the author's own clinical practice.

Dr. Nand presents here a unifying theory of dream interpretation, which he suggests combines analysis with scientific methodology. Nand agrees with much in Freud's sexual theories, but argues that these must be modified with the additional contributions of Jung and Adler. There may be food for thought here, but I confess that I cannot seem to get any kind of intellectual handle on this lazily written and poorly edited grabbag of psychoanalytic dream theories.

**Nashe (Thomas). The Terrors of the Night. Or, A Discourse of Apparitions.** 38p. Johan Danter. London, 1594.

A tale of a series of visions and dreams that appeared to an upper-class Englishman during an extended bout of illness. Many of these dreams and visions, it seems, were of a sexual nature, portions of which would warm the resolve of any good Freudian. While experiencing these sexual fantasies, the good gentleman sees a bevy of female devils dressed as nuns. One nun is just about to jump into bed with him when a neighbor has the bad grace to end this phase of the dream by sending forthwith a pouch of medicinal herbs. The gentleman takes the potion, which cures him of both dreams and visions. But, alas, he dies raving a few days later.

Nashe, an entertaining writer, also authored such intriguing titles as The Anatomy of Absurdity and An Almond for a Parrot. Certainly he was no prude. Still, Nashe's writings only go to show that in Elizabethan England, as in most other times, one is expected to pay for sexual transgressions, even those experienced during the dream state. A final quote from Thomas Nashe, "A dream is nothing else but a bubbling scum or froth of the fancy, which the day hath left undigested."

**Natterson (Joseph M.) & Gordon (Bernard). The Sexual Dream.** 212p. Crown. N.Y., 1977.

The authors, one a San Francisco psychoanalyst, offer the reader over fifty sexual dreams reported by contemporary men and women in all walks of life. These dreams are interpreted in relationship to the personal sexual problems of the dreamer, the dreamer's relationship to his or her own intimate network of family and friends, and finally, to that dreamer's interrelationship with the world at large.

The authors see in sexual dreams, not only the erotic, but a deeper meaning which may help in understanding who the dreamers are and what they really want out of life. The book closes with suggestions for the reader for working with his or her own sexual dreams.

**Natterson (Joseph M., editor). The Dream in Clinical Practice.** 498p. notes, bibliography, index. J. Aronson. N.Y., 1980.

Beautifully written, highly authoritative and brilliantly presented collection of twenty-eight studies by leading authorities. Certainly required on the bookshelf of every clinician. Natterson's collection is most probably the best there is in the last thirty or so years.

The book itself is divided into four categories: the first deals with the clinical theory of dreams, the second centers upon the dream in various psychopathological states, the third is devoted to the use of the dream in special therapeutic situations, and the final part deals with the approach to dream therapy by different schools of thought and in differing contexts.

It is difficult to single out one or two leading papers; all are excellent. This reviewer was particularly taken with the study of dreams in psychosomatic states and a study of REM sleep and nightmares. There are also fascinating reports on the dream in situations of sexual disfunction.

This book is indeed so important that I must include at the end a full listing of each paper and its author: "The Manifest Dream and its Latent Meaning" by Louis Breger; "Dreams in Which the Analyst Appears as Himself" by Robert D. Gillman; "The Dream as

A Curative Fantasy" by Roy M. Whitman; "A Collaborative Account of a Psychoanalysis Through Dreams," anonymous; "The Dream in Schizophrenia" by John S. Kafka; "The Dream in Manic-Depressive Psychosis" by Ping-nie Pao; "The Dream in the Depressive Personality" by Walter Bonime with Florence Bonime; "The Dream in Dissociative States" by Stephen S. Marmer; "The Private Language of the Dream" by Ramon Greenberg and Chester Pearlman; "The Dream in Obsessive States" by Arnold Namrow; "The Dream in Phobic States" by Sydney L. Pomer and Robert A. Shain; "The Dream in Psychotherapy" by Robert Langs; "The Dream in Regressed States" by John E. Gedo; "The Dream in Acting Out Disturbances" by Doryann Lebe; "The Dream in Psychosomatic States" by Harold Levitan; "Perverse Symptoms and the Manifest Dream in Perversion" by Charles W. Socarides; "The Dream in the Treatment of the Disadvantaged" by Frank M. Kline; "The Dream in Traumatic States" by Harold Levitan; "The Dream in the Suicidal Situation" by Robert E. Litman; "Nightmares" by Claude T.H. Friedmann; "The Dream in Psychoanalysis" by Samuel Eisenstein; "The Dream in Jungian Analysis" by Joseph L. Henderson; "The Dream in Analysis of Existence" by Werner M. Mendel; "The Dream in Brief Psychotherapy" by Marquis Earl Wallace and Howard J. Parad; "The Dream in Analytic Group Therapy" by Martin Grotjahn; "The Dream in Group Psychotherapy" by Joseph M. Natterson; "The Dream in Social Work Practice" by Marquis Earl Wallace; and, "The Dream in Sexual Dysfunction Therapy" by Roy M. Whitman.

**Needham (Joseph). Science and Civilization in China.** Vol. II. History of Scientific Thought. 697p. notes, glossary, bibliographies, index. Cambridge University Press. Cambridge, 1956.

Considering the antiquity of Chinese civilization, it is most surprising to this reviewer that while printing in China dates to the ninth century A.D., no significant book on dream interpretations seems to have been produced prior to the Ming Dynasty, or about 1562. That work, the Meng Chan I Chih (An Essay Explanation of the Principles of Dream Interpretation) by Chen Shih-yuan, is apparently available only in Chinese.

Needham points out that dream prognostication was practiced in China as in other ancient civilizations, "though it can hardly be said to have taken a very important place there." The Book of Rites of the Chou Dynasty (about the seventh century B.C.) makes brief mention of dream interpretation, recording that such tasks were in the Department of the Grand Augur, who had assistants in a lower grade charged with specialization in dream meanings.

One earlier work, the Thai-Phing Kuang Chi (Miscellaneous Records Collected During the Thai-Phing Reign Period), written about 981 A.D., does contain data on dream interpretation which Needham and others believe anticipated the theories of Freud by many centuries. Four chapters on dreams have been translated into German, though not English, by A. Pfizmaier in his paper "Aus dem Traumleben d. Chinesen," which appeared in the journal, sitzungsberichte d. k. Adademie d. Wissenschaften, Wien, Vol. 64, 1870.

Wolfram Eberhard, another noteworthy scholar of ancient China, points out in his paper "The Dream in China" [Presented before the Annual Meeting, Assn. for Asian Studies, April 1966], that the Chinese character for dream suggests "night' and carries the connotation of being covered, dark, unclear, or fuzzy. Traditional Chinese dream theory seems, according to Eberhard, to be an extension of Chuang-tse's saying, "The true man of old times has no dream during the night and no fear when he wakes, because his food is simple and his breathing deep."

While the pragmatic Chinese may argue that dreams are connected with food and eating, more mystical Chinese relate them to the Yin/Yang concept. If the female power (Yin) is powerful, one dreams of passing through great fires, light, and heat. On the other hand, other mystics find dream interpretation in the Five Elements, for example, "If the sun enters the womb, a son will be born; if the moon enters the womb, it will be a daughter."

In doing research in contemporary Taiwan, Eberhard discovered that the most common dream book being sold in Taipei bookstalls was a book ascribed to the eleventh or twelfth century B.C., but actually appeared to him to have been produced during the more recent Ming or Ching era.

In an attempt at direct experimental research, Eberhard also reports on an analysis of seventy-five dreams collected from college students in present-day Taipei. He found that deities were rarely mentioned and that the dead played no significant role. He compared the differences of the dreams of girls from boys, concluding that boys' dreams "are often expressed in an indirect or symbolic way." In a comparison between dreams of ancient China (gleaned through a review of the literature) and those dreams of modern Chinese, the author concluded that "The main difference between the earliest and the latest dreams seems to be that the role of the supernatural and of guilt feelings has decreased and that of fear and worry has increased."

While traditional Chinese culture seems to have paid little serious regard to dreams, the Chinese Communists today may be taking a new look, particularly in the area of lucid dreaming. A report on recent investigations among Peking university students may be found in Myrna Walters and Robert K. Dentan's study on lucid dreaming among the students of Han University (Lucidity Letter, vol. 4, no. 1, 1985). Dr. Dentan has been so impressed by the progress made in lucid dreaming techniques by the Chinese, that in a later book review he suggested it as a promising alternative to the Senoi technique.

**Nicoll (Maurice). Dream Psychology.** 194p. biblio. Frowde. London, 1917.

Early attempt to propound the dream concepts developed by Carl Jung. The author states, "The rebirth symbolism of dreams has been very badly mishandled by the Freudians . . . " Reprinted in 1979, but largely dated by later research, and of limited value today.

**Nocturnal Revels: Or Universal Interpreter of Dreams and Visions.** 263p. Barker & Son. London, [1805?]

Early views on the nature, causes, and uses of dreams, with examples drawn largely from the Bible and ancient history. Part II includes dreams of famous people, from antiquity to 18th century England. The book concludes with a dictionary of dream symbols (pp. 134-261), containing not a few quaint interpretations of their meaning. Primarily of historical interest.

**Noone (Richard). Rape of the Dream People.** 212p. illus., index. Hutchinson. London, 1972.

A biography of Pat Noone, brother of the author, who was lost in Malaya during the Communist insurgency. Pat (christened Herbert Deane Noone) received a "double-first" in history and anthropology in 1930 from Corpus Christi College at Cambridge, then accepted a job as field ethnographer at the Perak Museum at Taiping in Malaya.

It was while engaged in this work that he became acquainted with the Senoi tribe and observed the role of dreams in their culture. In that same year (1934), he returned to England to lecture the Oxford/ Cambridge Joint Faculty of Anthropology on "The Dream Psychology of the Senoi Shaman." The same lecture was given at the Musée de l'Homme in Paris.

The actual text of the lecture is lost, but is reported to deal with the dreams of the related Temiar tribe in which the dream is a spiritual experience, so great in significance that few important decisions are made by the group without one of the members having had a dream that pointed to that course of action. Temiar children are encouraged to talk about their dreams, and their children have special dream experiences not recorded in Western cultures.

Richard Noone writes of his brother's first meetings with Kilton Stewart and their joint investigations into Temiar dreamwork. Stewart sought to employ Temiar dream psychology as an instrument of socialization, while Pat Noone directed his efforts towards an understanding of the role of the dream in Senoi society and its use in shaping the whole pattern of the lives and culture of these people. Rape of the Dream People is one of the few sources outside those written by Kilton Stewart in support of claims that dreams played a unique role in Senoi life and culture.

**Normand (Camille le). Napoleon's Complete Dream-Book.** 192p. Robert M. de Witt. N.Y., 1872.

One of the most popular nineteenth century dream

dictionaries, spiced throughout with a hodgepodge of warnings, secret meanings, and prognostications. Some of the meanings seem to have originated during the age of Artemidorus, though many reflect the dream chapbooks so common in Europe during the Middle Ages. If one dreams of eyelids or eyebrows, we are told, "It predicts happiness in love matters and acquisition of wealth." To dream of a dragon, on the other hand, indicates "meeting some great man."

All this makes for entertaining, if silly, reading. The wide popularity enjoyed by this particular book (translated into five languages) makes it an important historical source for those interested in the development of pre-Freudian dream symbolism, as well as the mores of the common, and not too common, dream reader during the 18th and 19th centuries.

**Oaklander (Violet). Windows to Our Children. A Gestalt Therapy Approach to Children and Adolescents.** 335p. biblio. Real People Press. Moab, Utah, 1978.

There is a brief six page discussion of utilizing children's dreams in treatment. Oaklander describes the problems of getting children to tell their dreams, reporting excellent results in this area by having the children read a child's book on dreams as an entry point to revelation of their own dreams [Refer to the index for list of children's books about dreams]. Oaklander gives several examples of the dreams of children whose fathers were in a special alcoholic treatment program. In each case the dream revealed the child's sense of that family's crisis.

**O'Flaherty (Wendy Doniger). Dreams, Illusion and Other Realities.** 361p. notes, bibliography, index. University of Chicago Press. Chicago, 1984.

A fascinating discussion of the relationship between waking consciousness and the dream state as viewed in the philosophy and folklore of classical India.

Dr. O'Flaherty compares Western thinkers ranging from Plato to Freud and Piaget with traditional Indian schools of thought. She argues that where Western concern with the nature and importance of the dream may be summed up by the word "obsession," the Indians take a much lighter, though perhaps deeper and more fulfilling interest in the dream, in which myth becomes one with reality, and reality is never more than a myth dreamed. From her viewpoint as an Indologist, the author writes that modern depth psychology is possibly the closest to the Indian concept of the dream.

O'Flaherty surveys the philosophical and psychological dimensions of Vedic, Buddhist, and Puranic texts. She applies modern interpretative techniques to the dreams recorded in Indian folklore, fables, legends, and myths. In the thousand year old collection of Sanskrit narratives called the Yogavasistha, as is true with much of the literature of this genre, tales and dreams are intermixed. No clear distinction is made between the dreaming and the waking state. Here one may find telepathic dreams, shared dreams, and dreams within dreams. Dr. O'Flaherty introduces us into a world of fantasy and myth, and of dreams, in a presentation that should delight every dream romantic, folklorist, and Jungian scholar.

**O'Nell (Carl W.). Dreams, Culture, and the Individual.** 88p. biblio., index. Chandler & Sharp. San Francisco, 1976.

Introductory monograph viewing dreams in a cross-cultural context. Use of anthropological sources to examine dreams as manifested in different cultures is useful but too brief for serious research. A bibliographic essay at the end is helpful.

**Oppenheim (A. Leo). The Interpretation of Dreams in the Ancient Near East.** 186p. illus. [Transactions of the American Philosophical Society, New Series, Vol. XLVI, Pt. 3] Philadelphia, 1956.

A thorough Orientalist's study of the role played by dreams in the long dead civilizations of the Near East, based upon translations of those cuneiform tablets still extant. Dr. Oppenheim begins with a brilliant survey of the scholarly literature available on the dreams of the early Hittites, Mesopotamians, Sumerians, Akkadians, and Egyptians from the fifteenth century B.C., through the Christian era. Many of these he traces to adapted versions which appeared in the Old Testament of the Bible.

The principal effort in this study involves the author's careful translation of fragments from an Assyrian Dream Book dating to the ninth century B.C. From the literature that survives, it would appear that dream reports in the ancient Near East concerned dreams as revelations of a deity, which might or might not require interpretation; dreams revealing the mental or bodily state of the dreamer, including illnesses; and, dreams of prophecy.

One problem in historiography is that most of these early dream reports are recorded in royal inscriptions and reports, and there is very little relating to citizens of lesser rank. In many of these civilizations, dreams were considered a royal privilege. Reports of incubated dreams are rare, although Dr. Oppenheim does point out that they do appear where kings, facing an emergency, are reported to have resorted to divine help or advice through dream incubation. He traces this aspect through the early Hittite use of incubation to later evidence of it in the Bible, where we encounter the dream of Solomon in Gideon (I Kings 3:5), and that of Daniel in the Legend of Aght.

Interestingly, we find no evidence of a tendency for priests to receive revelations via the dream. Kings, on the other hand, offtimes made extensive use of "message dreams" to guide their actions and, in some cases, as a justification for royal usurption. The autobiography of the Hittite King Hattushili, dating to the thirteenth century B.C., contains the most ample use of dream stories in any records that survive. In that compilation, King Hattushili used his message dream from the goddess Ishtar to justify his usurption of the throne.

The Assyrian Dream-Book, the work with which this study is primarily concerned, is essentially an "omen-text," rife with such admonitions as "He who cuts down a poplar tree will have peace of mind." In rare instances there occur dream symbols, almost all having to do with progeny. Those reflecting the unconscious, however, appear to be extremely rare. We do find numerous dreams relating to urine, fish, fowl, and water. The urine/water dreams, suggests Dr. Oppenheim, relate primarily to progeny dreams, and may be equated with semen. There is also mention of flying dreams, concerned primarily with meetings with the dead, or walking on "heavy" or "light" water.

The author cautions that most of the translated material does not lend itself readily to modern techniques of dream interpretation. Many so-called "evil dreams," representing nightmares and disturbing dreams, are absent, since there was a tendency not to record these. Similarly, the author suggests that linguistic difficulties relating to special nuances and connotations have never been resolved, and conclusions drawn from these fragments would be most tentative at best.

There is a section devoted to early dream interpreters, particularly those who specialized in interpreting enigmatic dreams and those charged with dispelling or removing the evil consequences of a dream through one or another form of magic. One recorded method for ridding one of the consequences of an evil dream was to transfer it to a lump of clay, then throw the clay into a pond. The interpreter and dreamer would watch while the water gradually dissolved the clay. Most dream interpretations, however, consisted of attempts to interpret the message to the dreamer from a deity, couched in the form of a riddle, and almost always, referring to the future.

It is more than possible that the early tradition of dreams in the ancient Near East led directly to the wealth of dream interpretation works produced by Arabic scholars in the first centuries after the birth of Christ. A lineal descendant in dream interpretation was Muhammad ibn Sirin, of the eighth century A.D. Sirin was celebrated for his interpretation of even the most complicated of dreams. Dr. Gustave E. von Grunebaum, in a brief note on Sirin (Psychoanalytic Review, Vol. 30, 1943, pp. 146-147), reports several interesting examples of Sirin's interpretative skills. In one case ibn Sirin once explained a man's dream that he was ploughing a barren field by the fact that the man kept aloof from his wife. In another, he explained an ostrich that had been grinding wheat in a man's dream as relating to the man's problem with a slave girl whom he had been hiding from his lawful wife.

Unfortunately, I know of no study of the Arabic dream interpretation tradition in the centuries following the birth of Christ to match Dr. Oppenheim's scholarly explorations into the realm of ancient Near Eastern dream texts. This work includes a faithful translation of the oldest recorded dream, the Dream of the

Egyptian King Thutmose IV, some 1500 years before Christ. That dream dreamed at midday in the shadow of the Sphinx, was reported as a prophetic dream in which the god, Harmakhis-Khepri-Re-Atum, gave him the crown of both Upper and Lower Egypt, ending with, "Behold, I am with you. I am your guide."

Fascinating as well was the twelfth century B.C. dream of King Tanutamun. In this incubation dream, King Tanutamun dreamed of two serpents, one on his right, the other on his left. He dreamed that he awoke, wondering suddenly where his serpents had gone. The gods then informed him that it was necessary for him to claim his rightful throne, Upper and Lower Egypt, represented by the serpents, and he dreamed further that he acquired these possessions with the support of the multitudes. The tablet recording this dream ends with King Tanutamun's observation, "True indeed is the dream; it is beneficial to him who places it in his heart but evil for him who does not know it."

Dr. Leo Oppenheim has performed a major service with this contribution to ancient dreamlore and interpretation, all the more so since the early traditions in these civilizations directly influenced Arabic scholars of dream interpretation centuries later. It was their early works which led ultimately to the art of dream interpretation in our Western World.

**Osborn (Arthur). The Future is Now. The Significance of Precognition.** 254p. index. Univ. Books. N.Y., 1961.

Fifty-four cases of precognition, including twelve on dreams. Dreams discussed are concerned with warnings, impending death, knowledge of trivial events, and one dream projection predicting the length of World War II. The final section of the book consists of a parapsychological analysis of this phenomena.

**Oswald (Ian). Sleeping and Waking. Physiology and Psychology.** 232p. notes, tables, index. Elsevier. Amsterdam, 1962.

Academic work by research psychologist, with emphasis on physiological aspects. One chapter on dreams, touching on REM studies and dream modification.

**Oswald (Ian). Sleep.** 157p. graphs. index. Pelican Original. 1966.

Physiological and psychological aspects of sleep explained by an experimental psychologist. Dream analysis emphasizes laboratory experimental work in the 1950s and 1960s. A limited bibliography included. Analytical and academic.

**Ouspensky (Peter D.). A New Model of the Universe.** 476p. index. Knopf. N.Y., 1948.

One of the major efforts by this Russian-born mystic who has commanded a wide following for many years. One chapter (pp. 242-273), "On the Study of Dreams and on Hypnotism," presents a nonpsychoanalytical interpretation of dreams based on yoga and Hindu concepts, and suggests a system for dreaming not too far removed from present lucid dreaming techniques.

**Owen (Robert Dale). Footfalls on the Boundary of Another World.** 528p. notes, index. J.B. Lippincott & Co., Philadelphia, 1868.

An early attempt at a more scientific study of parapsychological science by a onetime congressman and American minister to the Court of Naples. Mr. Owen examines various aspects of what he calls "magneto-psychological character," treating ghosts and apparitions, the unexplained and miraculous, and the strange nature of dreams and sleep.

The dream chapter is extensive, covering from pages 137 to 209. Mr. Owen narrates precognitive dreams of Britons not generally recited elsewhere, particularly those relating to imminent murder or death. These include one noteworthy dream predicting the Indian Mutiny of 1858. This chapter is more a compilation of memorable dreams than any attempt at detailed study. The author suggests we reject the common theory that dreams are "mere purposeless wanderings of a vagrant imagination," substituting this dogma with further research.

**Palombo (Stanley R.). Dreaming and Memory. A New Information-Processing Model.** 237p. biblio., index. Basic Books. N.Y., 1978.

The dream seen as serving an information processing function, requiring a fusing of traditional techniques of Freudian dream therapy with modern laboratory facilities. Palombo argues that the dream censor substitutes meaningless day residue in order to cloak traumatic experiences, throwing up defenses that can be pierced only by the mechanism of the "correction dream." After a dream has been both reported and interpreted during analysis, a correction dream occurs, which is the result of the process of assimilating the previous dream report and interpretation. This correction, the author writes, functions as a tracer, carrying the interpretation back to specific locations in the memory where it is matched with the original dream. Polombo contends that the new dream will point to a solution of the patient's problem.

The correction dream is normally accompanied by very little anxiety, however. As a result, the dream is likely neither to awaken the dreamer, nor to be remembered by him. On the other hand, the correction dream can be identified when the dreamer is awakened during REM sleep in a laboratory environment.

Palombo's theory is refreshing, and his initial evidence is promising. But Palombo's greatest task lies neither in the laboratory nor with the pen. He must convince the working psychoanalyst to remove himself during portions of therapy to the laboratory, and to abandon from time to time the womb-like safety of his office and the satisfying setting of the traditional couch.

**Parker (Derek & Julia). The Compleat Book of Dreaming.** 223p. illus. Harmony Books. N.Y., 1985.

This outsized book is subtitled, "An Illustrated Guide to Remembering and Interpreting Your Dreams." Following a brief general discussion of dreams and dream theory, the authors introduce us into a beautifully illustrated, if less informative, dream dictionary, containing some fifteen hundred "dream themes, symbols, and images."

The authors advanced to dreamwork after writing their last book, The New Compleat Astrologer. The Parkers and their publisher have put together one of the more attractively illustrated and designed books to come to this reviewer's attention in many years. If this is an example of the old-fashioned dream chapbook in modern dress, then we stand at the threshold of a new era in popularization.

**Pausanias. Description of Greece.** 6 Volumes. Translated by W.H.S. Jones, G.P. Putnam's Sons. N.Y., 1918.

This second century A.D. Greek geographer and travel writer has left us one of the most accurate and informative travel guides to ancient Greece, standing today as one of the few solid bridges of objective writing extant between the Christian and ancient Hellenic world.

Much of what we know today of Greek life, customs, religion, and myth derives from the ten travel books authored by Pausanias. Scattered throughout its pages are descriptions of temple cures and dream incubation practices, accompanied by a discussion of the importance of the dream in ancient Greek life and religion. Pausanias writes of many prophetic dreams, including those of Phaylus, Plato, and Pindar, some portending good, but many either death or ill fortune. There is much on the role of the dream in dictating the lives and decisions of not only Greek gods, but of Greek rulers as well.

Intermixed, the reader discovers many fragments of dreamlore. We learn, for example, that a shrine dedicated to Isis, the holiest Egyptian goddess in the Greek pantheon, was closed off to casual visitors. "None may enter the shrine," reports Pausanias, "except those whom Isis herself has honored by inviting them in dreams." Invitation to a holy temple via the dream apparently was not uncommon. Books such as those authored by Pausanias suggest that the dream played a role in Greek life and culture more important than in any other large nation or geographic region, save perhaps, the Middle East.

**Pear (Tom Hatherly). Remembering and Forgetting.** 242p. notes, index. E.P. Dutton & Co. N.Y., 1922.

A substantial portion of this study by a professor of psychology at the University of Manchester in

England is devoted to imagery and dreams. The author discusses Freudian dream theories and, to a lesser extent, the contributions of Carl Jung. The principal effort here involves an examination of the dream views of W.H.R. Rivers, both a teacher and close friend of the author.

Rivers found great difficulty in reconciling Freud's theories of censorship, the alleged sleep-preserving function of the dream, and wish fulfillment, with certain dreams, particularly the nightmare and the undisguised sexual dream. He viewed the dream more in Adlerian terms, as an example of mental conflict seeking to resolve a particular problem. Rivers believed that the mental mechanisms at work in the dream are designed to bring about a primitive, less-developed solution to the problem than one arrives at during the waking period. Rivers postulates a "hierarchy of levels of potential behavior," each level controlling the one below it and, in turn, being controlled by the one above. Instincts, on the other hand, may throw these controls out of balance. Such emotions as anger, fear, and sexual arousal serve to mitigate against this control. The dream seeks through the use of concrete symbolic imagery to solve problems which we cannot face in everyday life.

In his chapter, "The Analysis of a Dream" Dr. Pear provides the reader with a detailed analysis of one of his own dreams, discussing the manifest content, sources of the manifest content, and an interpretation. This work is well documented, well written, and presents one of the clearest expositions of the theories of W.H.R. Rivers to appear in book form. Rivers' own arguments relating to Freudian dream theory are best explained in his article on this topic which appeared in the *British Journal of Psychology*, vol. xii, 1921, pp. 113-124.

**Pelton (Robert Wayne). The Complete Book of Dream Interpretation.** 151p. illus. Arco Publishing. N.Y., 1983.

Popular dream dictionary by professional free lance writer, with dream interpretations reminiscent of nineteenth century chapbooks, from which I suspect the author has lifted many of his interpretations of symbols. The saving grace to this compilation is an interesting introduction to popular dream interpretation, containing facsimiles of the title pages of many late nineteenth and early twentieth century dream chapbooks.

**Pereira (Benito). Comentariorum in Danielem Prophetam.** 495p. George Feraris. Rome, 1587.

Jesuit's scholarly study of the historiography behind the Dream Book of Daniel, along with its relationship to the moral doctrine on such works then established by the Catholic Church. The author points out that Daniel was a Jew [as was Christ], then proceeds to enumerate the various antichristian aspects of this work, particularly any prophecy resulting from dreams not divinely inspired.

**Pereira (Benito). De Magia, de Observatione Somniorum et de Divinatione Astrologica.** 324p. Ionnem Gymnicum. Cologne, 1612.

Book II of this theological treatise treats dream interpretations, particularly prophetic dreams, regarding them as contrary to the accepted teachings of the Church. Magic, astrological divination, and dream interpretation, argues the author, are but "adverse fallacies and superstitious arts."

In Book III, however, we discover this Jesuit does find merit in dreams of religious significance. "God," he writes, " . . . inspires dreams where he will, when he will, and in whomsoever he will." Pereira writes that certain senior monks in the early Church were responsible for "seeking out and testing the causes of certain dreams." He finds that dreams can be natural, of human origin, or divine. They may be caused by bodily afflictions, mental unrest resulting from extreme emotions such as love or hate, dreams occasioned by demons or the devil, or, dreams sent by God.

The author discusses the features indicating those dreams sent by God, but warns that as the devil may also produce prophetic dreams, great caution should be exercised as to the true cause and validity of the dream itself. Only those "divinely inspired and instructed" should interpret dreams, Pereira cautions. Carl Jung, in his discussion of the writings of Pereira, notes that while the author states that dream interpretation is reserved for those with the gift of the Holy Spirit, "It is obvious . . . that a Jesuit author could not envisage a descent of the Holy Spirit outside the Church" (See: Psychology and Religion, footnote, pages 19-21).

**Perera (Sylvia Brinton). Descent to the Goddess. A Way of Initiation for Women.** 111p. notes, biblio., index. Inner City Books. Toronto, 1981.

Modern dreams combined with mythology in a Jungian approach to the Sumerian goddess Inanna/Ishtar's journey to the underworld. An important work revealing woman's essential nature and the need to restore feminine values in today's masculine-oriented world.

**Perls (Frederick S.). Gestalt Therapy Verbatim.** Compiled and edited by John O. Stevens. 279p. Real People Press. Lafayette, Calif., 1969.

Major contribution to group therapy dreamwork by the father of modern Gestalt therapy. Perls establishes role-playing so that the dreamer shares and participates in every part of the dream, both real and fancied. The job of the group dream analyst is to fill the "emotional holes," which Perls viewed as portions of the psyche where problems and crisis from the past still festered as if they were open wounds.

These are edited transcripts from audiotapes of the dreamwork seminars conducted by Perls at the Esalen Institute, Big Sur, California between 1966 and 1968. The first session consisted of individual therapy sessions in a group dreamwork seminar setting. The second half of the book consists of transcriptions of the intensive workshop on playing roles in the dream. This is an important Gestalt contribution to dreamwork in group therapy, but suffers from indifferent editorial preparaton and the absence of any kind of table of contents or index.

**Peterson (William). Dreams. Our Judge and Jury.** 48p. A.R.E. Press. Virginia Beach, Virginia, 1951.

Early monograph outlining the Edgar Cayce method of dream interpretation, stressing the value of dreams in personal development and good health.

**Piaget (Jean). Play, Dreams and Imitation in Childhood.** 296p. index. Norton. N.Y., 1962.

The original French edition of this work was titled, La Formation du Symbole (1950), which is perhaps a better title than that given in the English edition. This book details a Geneva psychologist's studies of symbolism in the first years of a child's development. Those sections concerned with dreams cover secondary symbolism in dreams, accompanied by attempts to relate children's dreams through an analogy between dreams and children's games. These sections regrettably are few, and form only a small portion of this serious work.

**Pierce (Frederick). Dreams and Personality.** 337p. index. D. Appleton & Co. N.Y., 1931.

Professional psychologist's study designed to compare the waking with the dreaming personality of nine pairs of subjects. Those individuals and dreams selected by Dr. Pierce were drawn from his collection of over 1,000 dreams of 204 individuals in all stations of life. From eight to ten manifest dreams are given for each subject, followed by associations (i.e., the dreamer's post-dream ideas and emotions attached to the dream), ending with Dr. Pierce's analysis.

The sections of associations following individual dreams are too brief perhaps, and there is nowhere any indication that Dr. Pierce, a psychologist, sought to penetrate resistances or provide an interpretation in depth for any one dream. Significantly, a positive therapeutic effect did occur in some cases in spite of Pierce's reluctance to engage in direct therapy. Dr. Pierce found that the dream personalities were different from those exhibited during the waking states in ten men and ten women, while they were alike in the two remaining men and six women.

Through a review of his own data, the author concluded that his researches supported Freudian dream theories with the exception of the role of wish fulfillment, which he states was disproved. "There are many hundreds of elaborately associated dreams in my records," the author concludes, "which show neither wish fulfillment, nor compensation, nor concern with the instincts of hunger or love, and yet may reasonably be interpreted without recourse to the theory of resistance or censorship."

Pierce believed that dreams have a purpose. None are accidental. For some, dreams point to unresolved difficulties; for others, they serve as a release of creative expression; while in still others, dreams may act as an escape valve or warning of improper conduct, or of character flaws.

**Pinticart de Wessely (Elcira). Mi vida nocturna.** 140p. Ed. Universitaria. Santiago de Chile, 1976.

Collection of the dreams of a Chilean literary figure describing lucid dreams, dreams of precognition, and of astral travel. Includes a collection of beautiful dream sketches and drawings done by Elcira Pinticart.

**Pötzl (Otto, et al.). Preconscious Stimulation in Dreams, Associations, and Images. Classical Studies.** Introduction by Charles Fisher. 156p. illustrations, notes. [Psychological Issues, volume II, no. 3, monograph, 7] International Univ. Press. N.Y., 1960.

First English translation of an important early experimental study on dream imagery. The major portion of the book contains a translation of Pötzl's 1917 paper on induced dream images (pp. 41-120), preceded by Fisher's detailed analysis of the value and influence of this research. The 1924 paper on the utilization of unnoticed impressions in association, authored by Jakob Teller and Rudolf Allers, covers pages 121-150. Dr. Fisher has also included a bibliography of early research in this area.

Pötzl, a Vienna research professor and psychiatrist, undertook his work after observing patients suffering visual disturbances due to brain injuries. He began with the assumption, previously noted by other scientists, that visual stimuli not consciously perceived during the original viewing, sometimes appear as after-images. Pötzl also contends that while central vision may be a conscious process, those images arising in peripheral vision are normally excluded from the conscious mind.

Four experiments were conducted by Pötzl on preconscious stimulation in dreams. Colored slides and photographs were presented to induce dream images and these were compared with subjects' sketches of their dreams. Pötzl concluded that the visual dream images of normal patients were essentially the same in form and content with the visual errors in conscious patients suffering from agnosia. Utilizing a machine designed to present quickly-flashed pictures, he also demonstrated that portions of the picture would be registered "outside" the subject's consciousness, but would reappear in the consciousness after a delay of minutes or sometimes hours. Pötzl considered that this subliminal stage, during which these peripheral images appear to consciousness, is identical to that in dreams and hallucinations. Additionally, the memory of such images is often distorted, a distortion which Pötzl suggests resembles the condensations, displacements and symbolic transformations that Freud called dreamwork. Pötzl concluded that while consciously perceived visual images are excluded from dreams, subliminally registered peripheral images provide the raw materials for the dream. Furthermore, Pötzl suggests that the dream is a product of the interaction of sensory, motor, and symbolic stimuli, accompanied by "a general reintegration tendency of inhibited acts," which Pötzl equates with Freud's principle of wish fulfillment.

The Allers/Teller paper was influenced by the earlier

work of Pötzl, but centers on experiments with imagery rather than dreams. Their efforts focused on the laws that control the emergence of the "unnoticed" in visual stmuli, and the form in which the unnoticed image eventually appears. While Allers and Teller validate much of the earlier work done by Pötzl, the authors concluded that unconscious factors and repression played no part in what was consciously perceived and not perceived.

**Pontalis (J.B.). Frontiers in Psychoanalysis. Between the Dream and Psychic Pain.** 224p. biblio., index. International Universities Press. N.Y., 1981.

Prominent French psychoanalyst writes a thoughtful and thorough review of Freudian theory, treating the "character" of the dream as distinct from its content. The dream must be considered in its entirety, as a separate entity, rather than having one examine its parts. Pontalis, trained as a philosopher as well as a psychoanalyst, immersed himself for many years in existentialism, and his writings reflect this in the articulate, if sometimes complex, exposition in which he seeks to balance the two, particularly in merging abstract values with clinical concepts.

**Popper (Josef). Phantasien eines Realisten.** Reissner. Dresden, 1899.

Popper is remembered today primarily as a writer whose theories of the dream were closely parallel to those of Sigmund Freud. His book, in fact, antedated Freud's by several months. Written under the pseudonym, Lynkeus, Phantasien eines Realisten, has never been translated in its entirety into English. Popper, an engineer turned sociologist, appears to have advanced past Freud's theories in at least the cultural area. One chapter of his book was translated as Dreaming Like Waking, which was published by A.A. Brill in 1947. Another portion was translated by Saul Rosenzweig as an appendix to his article on the life and contributions of Popper in Psychoanalysis and the Social Sciences, Vol. V, pp. 9-50. N.Y., 1958.

**Pratchenko (Paul). Dream Riddles. Fragments of Daydreams and Nightmares.** 64p. illus. Simon & Schuster. N.Y., 1979.

Essentially a collection of interesting art by the artist/author, with very little written descriptions. Those interested in art symbolism in dreams may want to immerse themselves in this collection. To some it may appear more "artsy-craftsy" than informative. Perhaps it's a matter of taste.

**Prescott (F.C.). Poetry and Dreams.** 72p. Four Seas Press. Boston, 1912.

Dreams in the poetry of Shelley, Byron, Scott, George Elliot, Milton, Goethe, and others, related to the early contributions of Freud.

**Price (Nancy). Acquainted with the Night. A Book of Dreams.** 155p. Ronald. Oxford, 1949.

British actress' dream journal. Intelligent and lively compendium of dreams from the daily record of a sensitive and literate recorder.

**Priestley (J.B.). The Happy Dream. An Essay.** 35p. Limited to 400 signed and numbered copies. Whittington Press. Andoversford, England, 1976.

Literary raconteur denounces professional dream researchers who, he writes, "announce that dreams are simply the brain's garbage disposal, a ragbag of unwanted odds and ends, a swilling tour of the day's rubbish." Priestley finds that "People who believe this have lived so far in a much duller world than the one I know." Forget these rubbish dreams, he recommends, and concentrate on those handful of memorable dreams which cling to our memories year after year.

In this brief essay, Priestley discusses his favorite dreams, including erotic ones, and recounts a lifetime of his happy dreams. Our good author closes with a lament on the wears and tears of over seven decades of ordinary living, causing the intellectual images to dim, memories to fade, and bodily capacity to fail. One of the few treasures which seems to remain vivid and satisfying, however, is the dream. "How can we still say 'Only a dream'?" concludes Priestley, "This one brief dream towered above and outshone all the recent events of my old age. It has been the greatest gift that has lately come my way."

**Progoff (Ira). Depth Psychology and Modern Man.** 277p. notes, index. Julian Press. N.Y., 1960.

Progoff suggests an expansion of psychology from its largely medical domain to include metaphysical and philosophical values representing a holistic view of the universe. In his chapter titled, "The Dream of the Luminous Child," the author writes that dreams can convince the dreamer of the reality of the process of the deep unconscious. In his own dream experiences,

Progoff found no difficulty in understanding the holistic nature of man and his universe, and in integrating this ongoing process into the life of the dreamer.

In spite of the errors in modern science, the author writes that the "basic reality in man cannot . . . stay buried for long." Depth psychology requires that scientists balance the objective results of their experiments with their inner, unconscious experiences.

**Progoff (Ira). At a Journal Workshop. The Basic Text and Guide for Using the Intensive Journal.** 320p. Dialogue House Library. N.Y., 1975.

This holistic, self-betterment handbook contains exercises that can be practiced either in workshops or individually. It represents the practical application of many of Progoff's theories for advancing depth psychology into a new psychology of personal growth. The author recommends each individual keep a dream log as a method of recording "dream enlargement," Progoff's term for personalized dream interpretation and realization. Progoff recommends reviewing a dream log over several years, adding dreams which occurred before the dream log was begun, and fitting these together in a kind of "journal feedback process."

He suggests that we should not attempt to analyze these dreams. Forget the teachings of Freud, Jung, and Adler. Do nothing to make the dream or its symbolism "stand to reason." He states that to give an analytical interpretation would be to neutralize its power, and our dreams at this state are better left at the level of depth where they continue to expand their "lives" in the inner self.

Rather than analysis, Progoff recommends that we return to the place of our dreams in our experience, and reenter them, so that they may continue. "All our dreams are part of the moving flow of imagery that is continuously present at the depth level of the psyche," he advises. Once we return to our dream settings, the next step is to "sit in quietness," our journal open and our eyes closed, "sending our minds back over the movement of our dreams." This free association allows for present and past dreams to flow through an unconscious pattern in which we have a freedom of emotion in an equally free atmosphere of dreams.

So, according to Progoff, the dreamer begins to feel, rather than logically or rationally comprehend, the meaning of the dream. In bypassing the intellectual preconceptions of dreams, we flow with the emotions of our dreams, pausing now and then to refer to similar dreams in our dream log, eventually sensing a pattern. "The seriality of dreams," Progoff writes, "is the key factor with which we build the momentum that enables us to draw the dream process forward."

Progoff suggests we record in the dream log any dream which drew us into its atmosphere and is unlike any recorded earlier in the dream log. Show it as it is now. He argues that the fact that we are now focused on this dream is a significant message to us from our unconscious.

In a continuous process of intuitive and emotive reflection, balanced by regular referrals to one's dream log, the dreamer begins to enter his dream, "to get inside the movement of our dreams." The movement of our dreams, the author suggests, is not unlike that of a train, except that our dreaming gives us no ticket with the destination printed upon it, and our train has no conductor to announce our ultimate goal in advance.

Once fully within the movement of one's dream, Progoff points out that we are now in the state of "twilight dreaming." Here dreams continue themselves, may reappear in different settings; images, actions, and feelings flow on, just as in the case of dreaming while asleep. We flow with our dreams, then again record our experiences. These experiences constitute the "dream enlargement." Further reflection gives us a new view, and advances us to a stage where "we can think about them lucidly. Now the ideas that were merely intimations or hunches before can be considered critically and constructively."

Ira Progoff has realized more than satisfactory results from this technique in workshops conducted throughout the country. He has many advocates. The patience and resourcefulness required for undertaking this method of dreamwork on one's own, however, makes the process a demanding one. This workbook holds promise of rewards as a very interesting method of utilizing and fully understanding one's dreams. But the rewards do not hang easily like apples on the lower branches of a tree ready for the plucking.

**Quinn (Adrienne). Dreams. Secret Messages from Your Mind.** 128p. illus. biblio. Dream Research. Tacoma, Washington, 1981.

Introduction to dream interpretation by a dreamworker who conducts her own dream workshops throughout the United States. Dreams is used by Ms. Quinn as her instructional text. Although the beginner interested in dreamwork will find a number of helpful hints, one might suggest that the writer has sought to cover far too much in far too brief a space. Her presentation sometimes seems to confuse rather than illuminate.

**Radcliffe-Brown (A.R.). The Adaman Islanders.** 345p. London, 1933.

In discussing the islanders, Radcliffe-Brown notes that the medicine man was known as "The Dreamer," using his own dreams to cure the ill. The natives believed that sickness was caused by dreams, calling upon The Dreamer to contact the spirits, frequently through dreams, to pacify these unhappy spirits.

**Radestock (Paul). Schlaf und Traum.** 330p. Breitkopf & Hartel. Leipzig, 1879.

This book, by the author of other writings on habit, genius, and human psychology, is one of the genre of works on the relationship of dreams to psychosis that was extensively consulted and cited by Freud. Radestock was particularly interested in the influence of dreams on waking consciousness, while also observing the effects of external stimuli on dream content, i.e., the scent of flowers is transformed into a visual image of flowers in the dream. The author noted the frequency of anxiety dreams, and suggests that these and the more unusual and unsettling dreams are those most frequently remembered by patients. He writes that one's dreams "melt into a mad whirlpool of confusion," during which all associations are weak in both judgment as well as confirmation. Still, he concluded, our dreams reveal what we would not admit to ourselves in waking life.

**Randolph (Charles). How to Interpret Your Dreams.** 156p. Psychology Institute of America. N.Y., 1936.

**Rank (Otto). Psychology and the Soul.** Translated by William D. Turner. 195p. University of Pennsylvania Press. Philadelphia, 1950.

Otto Rank viewed the dream as a great spiritual

phenomenon as well as the "most subjective and mystical of all mental phenomena . . . " He attacks modern science's antispiritual orientation, which denies the meaningfulness of dreams, and concentrates too much on what dreams mean rather than accepting their spiritual essence as did primitive man. Psychoanalysis, he finds, stresses the dream but denies the soul. Primitive man interpreted reality in terms of his dreams, Rank suggests, while modern man permits the analyst to fit his dreams into current psychoanalytic ideology.

Drawing upon a wide variety of anthropological sources relating to dreams in primitive societies, Rank finds Freud's concepts wanting, and concludes that we have lost the spiritual value of dreams known to our more primitive forefathers. "The new respect for the dream" he concludes, "was Freud's only real contribution to the dream problem . . . ." Returning to the spiritual, Rank advises us that the dream itself is an interpretive phenomenon, containing all the bodily and psychic stimuli according to spiritual belief. This interpretation is the dream, Rank writes. Thus a causal explanation of the dream is not possible, principally because the dream can only be further interpreted, in an unending process.

A profound and illuminating writing in which Rank has much to contribute to our understanding of dreams. For twenty years Otto Rank was Sigmund Freud's personal secretary and one of his closest friends and staunchest advocates. The anti-Freudian stance is a trifle too emotionally charged, perhaps, but this is not surprising in a former pupil who finds his final break with his teacher both intellectually and emotionally traumatic.

**Rapaport (David). Seminars on Elementary Metapsy-**

**chology.** Edited by Stuart C. Miller. 163p. Stockbridge, Mass., 1959.

A verbatim transcript of seminars conducted with first year physicians and psychologists at the Western New England Institute for Psychoanalysis. This might better be called seminars on Freudian dream theory and therapy, for the entire seminar is predicated upon studies of Freud's The Interpretation of Dreams.

Topics covered are the differences between dream content and the dream as a thought form, the possibility of comparing dream-forgetting and everyday forgetting, determining a functional interpretation of dreams, the relationship between dream-work and interpretation, the relationship between the dream-wish and the day residue, and the relationship between the dream in neurosis and psychosis. In mimeograph form, but I would suspect that it could prove of value for teachers and students in their studies of Freud's dream theory.

**Rapaport (David, translator & editor). Organization and Pathology of Thought. Selected Sources.** 786p. notes, biblio., index. Columbia Univ. Press. N.Y., 1951.

Important German scientific papers in translation, including "Experimental Dreams" by Karl Schroetter; "Experiments on Symbolization in Dreams" by Gaston Roffenstein, and "Concerning Experimentally Produced Dreams" by M. Nachmansohn.

All are concerned in some measure with hypnosis in dreamwork, and each contains numerous examples with extensive annotations. The Schroetter and Roffenstein monographs deal primarily with isolated wishes and their symbolization, i.e., the coordination of drive and its ideational representation in a dream state.

The Nachmansohn paper seeks to advance these concepts further, integrating these dreams with the actual personality of the dreamer. The view here is that wishes and drives defy logical investigation, but may be manifest in dream analysis, particularly in their symbolic representation.

**Raphael. The Royal Book of Dreams.** London, 1830.

This was the great (most popular) dreambook of the 19th century. It was written by an astrologer and contained 1,024 dreams and oracles, interpreted by a method which Raphael called "Sephiromancy." In this system the dreamer need only write down two times five rows of zeros next to each other without counting them. According to the occult law of the soul, his hand will produce the correct interpretation through the pattern of zeros. A zero scale is included for guiding the dreamer. Certainly the earliest attempt, if specious, to quantify dream content analysis. This reviewer is indebted to Jolande Jacobi for the above exposition.

**Ratcliff (Arthur James J.). A History of Dreams. A Brief Account of the Evolution of Dream Theories, With a Chapter on the Dream in Literature.** 247p. Small, Maynard. Boston, Mass., 1923.

Well written general book, with emphasis on dreams in antiquity through the early Freudian and Jungian periods. Of historical interest.

**Rattray (R.S.). Religion and Art in Ashanti.** 414p. illus., index. Oxford, 1927.

In the chapter on dreams (pp. 192-204), Rattray deals

with dream interpretation and the reading of omens from dreams. Interestingly, the Ashanti dreamer is held responsible for any transgressions experienced in his dreams. A dream of committing adultery, for example, would require that the dreamer be fined as if he committed the act itself. There is a first-rate appendix by Dr. C.G. Seligman, who provides a modern psychoanalytic interpretation, comparing this with traditional Ashanti interpretations of their own dreams. He finds a remarkable parallel in the two approaches.

**Rawson (Wyatt). The Way Within. A Book of Psychological Documentaries.** 169p. Vincent Stuart Ltd. London, 1963.

Jungian orientation directed toward individual wholeness, based in part on P.W. Martin's interpretation of depth psychology. In one chapter, Dr. Rawson discusses dreams as spotlights, where the dream points to an aspect of existence that we are likely to forget or ignore when other aspects of our life run smoothly. He sees dreams as lifting "for a moment a part of the veil that covers the underlying motives of our actions . . . ."

In subsequent chapters the author expands on his concept that dreams are one of the best sources of revealing something "violent and explosive happening in the unconscious," even though the dreamer's outward existence may be placid and otherwise normal. Dr. Rawson gives numerous dream examples, most of which I found both illuminating and helpful. His chapter on "Self-knowledge and Dream Interpretation," contains interesting points on dream symbols and on the role of numbers in dreams.

This book may be difficult going for the layman not versed in Jungian terminology. Yet those who work at it will find The Way Within a fine guide to self-knowledge through the study of the dreams of generally well-adjusted people.

**Reed (Henry). Dream Realizations. A Dream Incubation Workbook.** 210p. Privately printed. Virginia Beach, Virginia, 1984.

This workbook has been effectively used by Dr. Henry Reed in conducting courses on dream incubation in co-operation with the Association for Research and Enlightenment, and in individual group seminars. The workbook requires twenty-eight days (and nights), and completion of the workbook sections sometimes needs from one to five hours of waking concentration for each week of dreams. Individuals seeking to undertake this workbook on their own are cautioned that the completion of the entire program requires desire, discipline, and dedication. But the rewards are well worth the effort.

**Reed (Henry). Getting Help from Your Dreams.** 143p. illus. Inner Vision Publishing Company. Virginia Beach, Virginia, 1985.

A well written, popular introduction to self-help through dreaming, authored by an innovative dream specialist with an established reputation among his peers for his creative work on dream incubation. This introduction teaches the beginner how to remember and record dreams, the techniques of dream incubation, and the art of realizing positive benefits from dreams. Interspersed in the text are Dr. Reed's comments on his own dream experiences, accompanied by a host of practical suggestions designed to aid the dreamer in achieving the most in mental, emotional, and spiritual health through dreams.

Henry Reed is one of a select few in modern psychology who can boast of more than two decades in dedication to exploratory, even revolutionary, dream research far removed from the laboratory experimental experiences that attract most professional psychologists with an interest in dream research.

As a clinical psychologist, Reed has specialized in providing dream therapy for other clinical psychologists and psychiatrists; in teaching, he has lectured extensively and outlined new courses on dreams for the Association for Research and Enlightenment. In addition to giving seminars throughout the country on dream incubation, Henry Reed also almost single-handedly edited and published a periodical devoted to dreamwork, the Sundance Community Dream Journal, which served as a leading forum for the interchange of ideas on dreams between professionals and laymen for several years. With Dr. Robert Van de Castle, Reed is currently editing and publishing the Dream Network Bulletin, a worthy successor to Sundance.

The biographical data given on Henry Reed in this review of his book is substantial, but not without purpose. Beyond the level of the more popularly known writers on dreams, there exists a small but very important group of dedicated professionals whose work is making a significant contribution to the field of dreams. Henry Reed is a leader among these, and his writings deserve wide circulation.

**Reich (Peter). A Book of Dreams.** 172p. Harper & Rowe. N.Y., 1973.

Son's partial biography of his father as seen through the eyes of a seven year old child. Peter Reich came upon the idea for this book while dreaming under sedation during an operation. The dream interlaces the book throughout and is used as the vehicle for the biography. Wilhelm Reich, the subject, was an internationally known psychiatrist who suddenly quit his professional work, bought a large tract of land in Maine, calling it Orgonon. There he "discovered" Orgone Energy, which he called life's energy, conducting experiments with a large electronic instrument he called an accumulator. Dr. Reich eventually died in an institution.

In his earlier career, Wilhelm Reich is remembered as the first analyst to appreciate that it might be possible and indeed necessary to treat patients by interpreting the nature and function of their character rather than their dreams. But this biography is not concerned with Reich's early contribution so much as his later emotional and intellectual disintegration, and the son's dreamwork, more as a vehicle in which the author sought to come to grips with his relationship with his father and with his father's eventual psychic dissolution.

**Reid (Clyde H.). Dreams. Discovering Your Inner Teacher.** 100p. Suggested Readings. Winston Press. Minneapolis, Minn., 1983.

Dream guide and workbook by a clergyman and Jungian psychotherapist. Solid, basic religious orientation designed to guide the dreamer to achieve self-discovery through dreaming. Chapters on unlocking your own dreams, symbols and archetypes, dream interpretation, how the dream can serve as the "inner teacher," and the role of dream-sharing groups show the dreamer how to rely on his or her inner resources in uncovering the meaning of a dream. An excellent entry into dreamwork for those seeking spiritual as well as personal enlightenment. Unfortunately the book is hampered by lack of an index, although it does include an informative section on suggested readings.

**Renard (Hélène). The Dream and the Naifs.** 332p. illus., biographies. Vilo Inc., Publisher. N.Y., 1982.

A collection of attractive, sometimes intriguing, paintings with dream motifs by 140 twentieth century painters of naive art. Included are the works of a number of lesser known artists from Yugoslavia, Haiti, Turkey, Czechoslovakia, France, and Brazil. Frequently photographs and biographies accompany examples of each painter's works.

The introduction by Vilém Stránský of Prague and the accompanying narrative sections are informative, though less impressive than is the art itself. This large coffee-table publication is designed to satisfy the emotional and aesthetic rather than the intellectual needs of the serious dreamworker. And, in this respect, it does a fine job.

**Rhine (Louisa E.). Hidden Channels of the Mind.** Foreword by J. B. Rhine. 292p. William Sloane Associates. N.Y., 1961.

The Rhine family, both husband and wife, have suffered their own tragic history in the field of ESP investigation. What started with such great promise, ended after many years of investigation with Duke University closing down Rhine's Parapsychological Laboratory and terminating effectively all financial support for this research.

While the Rhines' efforts were not primarily concerned with dreams, some investigation and reporting was made into telepathic dreams. In this book, Louisa Rhine seeks to explain [and defend] both her and her husband's years of investigation into ESP. Throughout are many instances of telepathic dreams recorded in the files of the laboratory.

Unfortunately, and this was certainly one of the basic criticisms of their laboratory, there is little substantiation and no evidence of controlled laboratory experiments. The book contains scant documentation and only a limited bibliography.

**Rhine (Louisa E.). ESP in Life and Laboratory.** 278p. notes, index. Macmillan. N.Y., 1967.

Includes commentary and investigations into telepathic dreams, both realistic and unrealistic. In the unrealistic dream, according to Rhine, the message is carried by the meaning of the fantasy rather than through exact imagery. The realistic dream on the other hand treats forms of experience, and can be both prophetic and telepathic. Dr. Rhine supplies a number of dreams which have come to the attention of the Rhine researchers into ESP, primarily those relating to telepathy.

**Richard (Jérome). La Théorie des songes.** 320p. Estienne. Paris, 1766.

**Ricoeur (Paul). Freud and Philosophy. An Essay on Interpretation.** Translated by Denis Savage. 573p. notes, index. Yale Univ. Press. New Haven, 1970.

Monumental explanation of Freudian theory, with extensive discussion of Freud's The Interpretation of Dreams, dreamwork, and the psychology of dreams. A basic work on the proper analytic reading of Freud. Well documented and indexed.

**Riffel (Herman). Your Dreams: God's Neglected Gift.** 118p. index. Ballantine. N.Y., 1981.

Christian minister's personal account of the importance of dreams. The reader is given Christian guidelines for dream analysis. Recommended for those with religious reservations about dreamwork and dream analysis.

**Rivers (W.H.R.). Dreams and Primitive Culture.** 28p. notes. Manchester University Press. London, 1918.

An early attempt at cross-cultural analysis before this term was coined. Dr. Rivers' monograph seeks to examine the psychological characteristics of the dream within primitive cultures, defining such characteristics as that mechanism by which the dream is produced. The analysis is designed to test the Freudian concept that the myth of a people comes into being through the action of laws very similar to those which produce the dream in the individual.

Dr. Rivers discusses the function of dramatization, symbolization, condensation, disguise, displacement, secondary elaboration, and censorship, and relates each to the dreams of primitive peoples. To allay the fears of those who might suggest that primitive cultures being so infinitely varied, "if you cast your net widely enough, resemblances are to be found for everything," Dr. Rivers draws his cases only from Melanesian and Papuan cultures with which he was intimately familiar.

The author concludes that the dream experiences in primitive cultures support most if not all of Freud's theories. He emphasizes the relationship between the myth and the dream in such societies. To the primitive, the myth occupies the place occupied by history and science in the civilized world. "The myth reveals the unconscious history of the race just as the dream reveals the unconscious history of the individual." He argues that the similarity between the dream and primitive culture manifests itself clearly when the unconscious past is presented to consciousness.

Dr. W.H.R. Rivers began his professional life as an anthropologist. His first major work, History of Melanesian Society, was published in two volumes in 1914. Shortly after the publication of this study, Dr. Rivers changed careers and became a psychiatrist. He is remembered as one of the first analysts to introduce the then pioneering work of Sigmund Freud to the English-speaking world.

This monograph represents the thinking of the author during his "Freudian period." He later altered his thinking and attacked the concepts of both Freud and, to a lesser extent, those of Carl Jung. Rivers' later views are given in the work that follows and are expressed as well in the books on dreams by Robert Graves and Tom Pear, also to be found in this bibliography.

**Rivers (W.H.R.). Conflict and Dream.** 195p. index. Harcourt, Brace & Co. N.Y., 1923.

Dr. Rivers writes that the dream is a product of mental conflict rather than wish fulfillment. He views the dream as an attempt to solve a problem for waking life, which may be successful, partially successful, or totally unsuccessful. Rivers utilizes the examples of the nightmare and the manifest sexual dream to contest Freudian theory, particularly wish fulfillment, censorship, and the sleep preservation function. Dr. Rivers is less critical of Carl Jung, although he does note that Jungian dream theories, not to mention the concept of the collective unconscious, have yet to be proven.

**Robert (W.). Der Traum als Naturnotwendigkeit Erklart.** 53p. H. Seippel. Hamburg, 1886.

The author constructs a theory of dreams based on the premise that normal dreams are concerned generally with events of recent waking life. He believed that problems resolved, or about to be resolved, were seldom the subject of one's dreams. Rather, the dream was concerned primarily with problems for which the dreamer had as yet no solution.

Robert suggested working with these dreams as a method of resolving immediate problems. Sigmund Freud acknowledged Robert's arguments, but suggested that Robert's thesis was not tenable since "indifferent memory images from our childhood appear all too frequently in our dreams." Freud called Robert's approach a "utilitarian theory of dreaming." Robert's theories closely parallel those later developed by Alfred Adler.

**Roberts (Ainslie) & Mountford (C.P.). The Dreamtime Book. Australian Aboriginal Myths in Paintings by Ainslie Roberts and Text by Charles P. Mountford.** Folio. 159p. Robert Hale & Co. London, 1974.

This large sized book contains seventy-six colored and black and white illustrations of the myths of Australian aborigines, each accompanied by a textual explanation. Topics like "The Ice Maidens" and "Cave of Fire" relating to oral traditions, myths, and folk tales, are only incidentally connected to the dream.

**Robertson (E.D.). Temiar Dream Songs From Malaya.** Folkways Record & Text. Album P. 460. N.Y., 1955.

Senoi related tribe. Recordings with text.

**Robinson (Stern) & Corbett (Tom). The Dreamer's Dictionary. The Complete Guide to Interpreting Your Dreams.** 285p. Taplinger. N.Y., 1974.

Lady Robinson, a New York scriptwriter, and the psychic Tom Corbett combined in "one year's research" to give us "the complete guide" to dream interpretation, explaining the meanings of over 3000 symbols. There are pitfalls to preparing a dream interpretation dictionary to cover all people at all times and in all mental states and psychic conditions. These become even more dangerous when one finds no sources listed for deriving the meanings, and when the authors see fit to cite astrological and psychic sources as major contributors to this work. The Dreamer's Dictionary was picked by the Psychology Book Club as a principal offering in 1974, which does not inspire me to subscribe to that club's membership.

Except where one is concerned with the ancient and classical dream dictionaries, and there with an arcane and scholarly approach, one is always on dangerous ground in this area. I am not certain any effort would be successful, no matter how detailed and exhaustive the research, and how careful the notations. Surely the exceptions for every dream meaning would exceed the meanings themselves. No plaudits here for a dictionary that could cause the beginning dreamer more harm than good, and which is hardly required by the specialist.

**Rogers (L.W.). Dreams and Premonitions.** 140p. Theo. Book Co. Chicago, 1923.

Primarily a collection of dreams of Americans during the first part of the 20th century, relating to dreams of premonition, dreams of the dead, and astral experiences. With a Theosophical orientation.

**Roheim (Geza). The Eternal Ones of the Dream. A Psychoanalytic Interpretation of Australian Myth and Ritual.** 273p. illus., map, index. International Univ. Press. N.Y., 1945.

By one of the pioneers of cross-cultural dreamwork. In this early study, despite the title, the emphasis is on totemism rather than on dreams. Dr. Roheim explains the title of his book, The Eternal Ones of the Dream, as an investigation into the immortality myths of Australian aborigines, which he views in Freudian terms, primarily as a denial of separation anxiety. The author does examine some dream facets in his cross-cultural investigation of circumcision, totemic myth, phallic ritual, fertility rites, the rainbow serpent, and the totem sacrament among the aborigines of Central Australia.

One of the more interesting chapters is on the relationship between myths and dreams, with a discussion of immortality in dreams and the dream mechanism as the nucleus of ritual and myth. The orientation is heavily Freudian, although the author does appear to struggle occasionally in his effort to reconcile his investigative data with accepted Freudian theories.

**Roheim (Geza). The Gates of the Dream.** 554p. notes, index. International Universities Press. N.Y., 1952.

A convincing argument that psychoanalysts should use anthropology in their work. Dr. Roheim's second argument, that one must be a practicing psychoanalyst to understand anthropology, has naturally made less headway among the body of the world's professional anthropologists. The author discusses the role of the dream in primitive society, animism, the use of the dream by shamans, the primitive idea of ogres and ghosts, and the role of dream, particularly the nightmare, in primitive mythology. He analyzes the manifest and latent meanings of the bear, water spirit, bird, water carrier, dragon, coyote, and a host of other symbols within a wide variety of cultures, with particular emphasis given to the aborigines of Australia.

The orientation is obviously Freudian. The author states that he was particularly influenced by the theories proposed in Sandor Ferenczi's Thalassa, which support Freud's observations that "The vagina is valued as the abode for the penis, it is the heir to the mother's womb." He also takes great stock in E.B. Tylor's thesis that the concept of gods in primitive cultures derives from animism, which itself is derived from the dream, as well as with Laistner's arguments that mythology is nothing more than the result of primitive nightmares.

Dr. Roheim sees life as a turning inward, and a journey "in time toward the past," a regression which includes a type of maturation faced with a congenital resistance to maturation. "We are born with a conflict between our older and more recent heritage, and something in us that is rather vaguely defined in psychoanalysis as the ego is the organic defense against this inherent conflict. This synthetic function underlies the other synthetic function of mediating between the id and the superego. The struggle is eternal, the results never stable."

Although the author has done a prodigious amount of research, I was disturbed by a weak index and the absence of a careful bibliography. While many cross-cultural professionals, particularly those concerned with dreamwork, tend to dismiss Roheim as too dogmatic and narrow in his theories, I found rewarding information here, especially in the areas of dream symbolism and in the importance of the role of the dream in many primitive cultures. I would have been happier had Dr. Roheim presented his massive research for what it is, rather than as a series of academic buttresses to substantiate his sometimes obtuse theories.

**Roheim (Geza, editor). Psychoanalysis and the Social Sciences. Vol. I.** 427p. Int'l Univ. Press. N.Y. 1947.

A noteworthy volume, expanding upon Geza Roheim's concepts of the relationship between psychoanalysis and anthropology. This pioneering series in cross-cultural analysis, contains one important article by Roheim on "Dream Analysis and Field Work in Anthropology." This forty page study is the basis for all important anthropological work in the purpose and methodology of dream research.

There is an informative introduction, tracing the first suggestion of the need for dream research by anthropologists to E.B. Tylor's Primitive Culture (London, 1903), which based a major theory of animism on dream life or primitive man's interpretation of dream life. Roheim follows by stressing C.G. Seligman's work on "type dreams" (tooth-losing dream, flying dream, and climbing dream) in his presidental address before the Royal Anthropological Institute in 1924.

To guide the anthropologist in the field, Roheim presents a research and investigative methodology for dream recording and interpretation, and follows with his own fieldwork examples made in Central Australia, giving seven dreams of a thirty-five year old native, followed by an analysis and discussion of dream associations. A major effort in a pioneering methodology.

**Roscher (Wilhelm Heinrich) & Hillman (James). Pan and the Nightmare.** 63;88p. Spring Publications. Irving, Texas, 1979.

Translation of Roscher's 1900 monograph on the pathological and mythological role of the nightmare in antiquity, with an introductory essay on the God Pan by James Hillman.

Hillman points out that Roscher, "more than any other classicist is responsible for having collected into one place the mythical and religious material of the ancient world, providing the ground for the scientific study of myth and symbol," in his multi-volume encyclopedia of Greek and Roman Mythology.

With his interest in comparative mythology, Roscher examines the nature and origin of the nightmare from such diverse sources as the ancient Greek and Roman physicians, discovers its roots in classical mythology, and traces the etymological designations and derivations of the nightmare. He also includes observations on the nightmare by the medical practitioners of his day. To which James Hillman has added the archetypal and psychological significance of the god Pan and his role in the nightmare, relating these to early concepts of masturbation, rape, and panic.

**Rose (Ronald). Living Magic: The Realities Underlying the Psychical Practices and Beliefs of Australian Aborigines.** 240p. illus. Rand McNally. Chicago, 1956.

Results of the field investigation designed to test ESP potential of aborigines in Central and East Coastal Australia by a husband and wife team. The investigators used the standard Rhine cards in their tests. Rose reported positive ESP results, and included in this work two appendices suggesting a methodology which, I suspect, would not meet modern experimental requirements. The expedition was financed in part by the Duke University Parapsychology Laboratory, and the book contains an introduction written by J.B. Rhine. The dream materials are haphazardly presented, and the conclusions strike this reviewer as questionable. There is no index.

**Rossi (Ernest L.). Dreams and the Growth of Personality. Expanding Awareness in Psychotherapy.** 217p. illus., biblio., index. Brunner/Mazel. N.Y., 1985.

Ernest Rossi writes books that are hard to be neutral about. This California Jungian analyst and clinical psychologist suggests theories and practical techniques unbound by the common boundaries established by both Jung and modern experimental psychology. His peripatetic mind ranges over the entire spectrum of mysticism, philosophy, science, and humanistic psychology, picking tidbits here and there, and mixing them in a form of alchemy Rossi calls the psycho-synthetic theory of dream formation.

As best I can tell, Dr. Rossi has formulated a method encouraging the expansion of the individual through self-awareness. This is accomplished by guided dream therapy. The principal vehicle Rossi utilizes to prove his thesis is the case study, including thirty-three dreams of a patient who, Rossi claims, was guided from "psychotic-like states to higher levels of awareness, love and individuality." Perhaps because of his California orientation [Rossi lives and practices in Malibu], the author believes that much of today's emotional turmoil stems from the individual's sense of alienation and loneliness.

In a certain sense Dr. Rossi follows good Jungian tradition by combining philosophical, psychological, mythological, and spiritual values in both theory and practice. This is all to the good, and Rossi's method certainly seems to work. I am less persuaded by his analysis of the nature and validity of his dream-protein hypothesis. He argues that dreaming causes psycho-physiological growth involving a synthesis or modification of protein structures in the brain, and that such action functions "as the organic basis for new developments in personality." This theory was originally proposed by Rossi in 1972, and, although he utilizes the works of Hartmann and certain REM researchers to bolster his thesis, it seems to me that Rossi is better positioned to continue producing stimulating new ideas, of which he is certainly capable, than complicating his arguments with propositions that are better left to laboratory investigators.

Dreams and the Growth of Personality was originally published in 1972. This new, revised edition, contains an additional chapter, reviewing more recent theories and experimental evidence relating to the dream. Parts of Rossi's writings will infuriate, parts even seem naive, but the whole of his contributions makes for a freshness and vitality that is more than enough to recommend this book.

**Rowe (Richard R.). Daydreaming Under Stress.** 97p. University Microfilms. Ann Arbor, 1963.

Doctoral dissertation at Columbia University in which the author established a series of controlled experiments on daydreaming. He found that the opportunity to daydream under stress resulted in significant decreases in heart rate, providing support for the drive-reduction model of the effect of daydreaming under stress. Corollarily, Rowe found no evidence to support Freud's contention that frequent daydreamers are likely to be more anxious.

**Rufus of Ephesus. On The Interrogation of the Patient.** [In Classical Greek] Edited by Charles Daremberg. Paris, 1879.

This early second century A.D. Greek physician exerted a great influence over Galen. Unfortunately most of his writings have been lost, although he apparently devoted considerable study to his patient's dreams.

Rufus suggests that all physicians ask their patients about their sleep habits, including any visions or dreams. He relates the case of Myron of Ephesus, a wrestler, who, although in apparent good health, recounted his dream: Myron dreamed that he was lying the entire night in a black marsh filled with fresh water. The next morning Myron experienced shortness of breath, feebleness, and chest palpitations while exercising. Shortly, he became unable to move his hands or feet and lost his power of speech. Not long afterwards, he died. Rufus suggests that Myron might not have died if he had paid attention to his dream, although the Greek physician's remedy (extensive bleeding to counteract the strain) may not have saved Myron either.

"I am fully persuaded," Rufus of Ephesus writes, "that ideas occurring in dreams, whether of good or bad significance to the individual, depend upon the humours in the body; and, further, that no full understanding of such ideas is possible without hearing what the patient has to say." I am indebted to Arthur J. Brock's translation in Greek Medicine (London, 1929, pp. 112-118), for this data on Rufus of Ephesus.

**Rycroft (Charles). The Innocence of Dreams.** 181p. notes, index. Pantheon Books. N.Y., 1979.

Noted British psychiatrist's review of recent REM and related experimental findings leads him to conclude that Freudian and Jungian dream theories do not measure up in light of modern scientific research. Rycroft, who reflects an ever-increasing consensus among practicing psychotherapists, suggests that the dream is actually a reflexive mental activity that allows the individual to communicate with himself. The author writes that dreaming is the sleeping form of imagination, which is a natural and normal activity of the self.

Rycroft finds the innocence of dreams reflected by the fact that the dreamer does not intend the dream. While the author concedes that the dreamer "knows more" than he does while awake, and may even dream dreams that result in guilt when remembered, still these dreams "lack knowingness, display an indifference to received categories, and have a core which cannot but be sincere and is uncontaminated by the self-conscious will."

Interestingly, while Rycroft seeks to feed the end product of much REM research into the equation forming his hypothesis of dreams, he ends up by suggesting that The Innocence of Dreams is more an attempt to marry Coleridge's theory of poetic imagination and Freud's theory of dreams than anything else.

**Ryff (Walther Hermann). Troumbüchlin.** 40;223p. Samuel Emmel. Strassburg, 1554.

Early translation and adaptation of Artemidorus by a German physician and mathematician.

**Sabin (Katherine). ESP and Dream Analysis.** 205p. index. Regnery Co. Chicago, 1974.

Attempt to combine ESP and related occult considerations with dreams and dreamwork. Special emphasis given to Jungian archetypes as manifested in dreams.

**Sacerdote (Paul). Induced Dreams.** Introduction by Erika Fromm. 179p. T. Gaus. Brooklyn, N.Y., 1967.

Dr. Sacerdote's book suggests a very effective method of psychotherapy designed to shortcut the process of prolonged psychoanalysis. He reports that he has been successful in this procedure for more than ten years. The heart of Dr. Sacerdote's method centers on the hypnotic induction of a series of consecutive dreams treating the same problem faced by the patient. These dreams are induced and dreamt while under hypnosis during the therapy session itself. The analyst guides the patient, step by step, from one dream to the next, until the patient is able to come to grips with his problem.

The author proposes that the psychoanalyst substitute hypnotically induced and guided dreams for free association, suggesting as well that dreams serve a duality of communicative functions: as a means of the patient's unconscious conversing with its preconscious, and also as a means of communicating with the patient's therapist.

The evidence mounted by the author is substantial. We find illustrative examples from Dr. Sacerdote's clinical practice, including one covering twenty-seven consecutive dreams dreamt by one patient. In his review of this work, Dr. Burton S. Glick writes that "It may eventually turn out that hypnotically induced and guided dreams are of infinitely greater therapeutic potential than naturally occurring ones."

While both Erika Fromm and Burton Glick highly recommend this book to all therapists willing to consider a new, possibly very useful approach to therapy, this reviewer finds no evidence that this has been the case. Another example of a strikingly fresh idea, buttressed by practical clinical evidence, gathering dust in a book whose printing numbered probably no more than 500 copies.

**Sadger (J.). Sleep Walking and Moon Walking. A Medico-Literary Study.** 140p. notes index. Nervous & Mental Disease Publishing Co. N.Y., 1920.

The author proposes that sleep walking as a method of wish fulfillment lies close to dream life, and that most sleep walking seems to take place in moonlight, particularly under the full moon. Dr. Sadger, a Viennese psychoanalyst, presents a series of clinical cases and the results of his research into literature in support of his contention. He argues that sleep walking fulfills the wishes of the day, while the dream fulfills those from childhood. A suggestive work rather than a conclusive one, and the portions related to dreams are secondary to that topic closest to the heart of Dr. Sadger, the sleepwalker.

**Sager (Clifford J.) & Kaplan (Helen S., editors). Progress in Group and Family Therapy.** 935p. notes. Brunner/Mazel. N.Y., 1972.

"The Use of Dreams in Gestalt Therapy" by James S. Simkin (pp. 95-104) provides a transcript designed to illustrate Gestalt principles and techniques in dream therapy.

**Samuels (Mike & Nancy). Seeing With the Mind's Eye. The History, Techniques and Uses of Visualization.** 331p. illus. Random House. N.Y., 1975.

An ambitious and beautifully illustrated book demonstrating the value and use of visual symbols and techniques in developing human consciousness. With numerous references to the visual aspects of dreams and dreaming, particularly their potential in healing.

**Sanctis (Sante de). Die Träume.** Translation by O. Schmidt. 286p. Halle, 1901.

A major study by an Italian pioneer in theoretical

and experimental dream research. Sanctis investigated the dreams of both normal as well as mentally disturbed individuals. He found that boys at age eleven dreamed frequently, while those at age six dreamed less so.

In a statistical analysis of the reported dreams of 165 men and 55 women, Sanctis found that women reported more frequent and more vivid dreams, while both sexes over the age of sixty-five reported they dreamed but rarely. He concluded that a loss of memory, less emotional stimuli, and dreams of more long past scenes, rather than recent events, were responsible.

Sanctis divided paranoiacs into three classes: those with systematized delusions, those with frequent hallucinations, and degenerates. The dreams of the first group resembled their delusions, the second class was distinguished by the complexity of their dreams; while the third by the vividness of dreams, by their delusions of megalomania, and by the influence of the dream on the individual during waking life.

Sanctis wrote a number of articles for professional journals on dreams, notably, "Psychoses et rêves," (Rapport au Congrès de neurol. et d'hypnologie de Bruxelles, 1897). He is the author of an earlier work in Italian on the relationship between the dream and epilepsy. His works had great influence on Freud. This work was originally published under the title, I Sogni, in Turin in 1899.

**Sanford (John A.). Dreams and Healing.** 164p. index. Paulist Press. N.Y., 1978.

Highly readable attempt to demonstrate the relationship between dreams and religious experience, authored by an Episcopalian clergyman with a Jungian orientation. There is a particularly interesting discussion of the role played by dreams and visions in the Bible and the first years of Christianity. The author also discusses the potential of healing dreams, both for the body as well as the "sick soul." Sanford illustrates his points with examples drawn from his own experiences in pastoral counseling, including a dream series on the healing value of dreams based on both a male and female not undergoing analysis.

**Sanford (John). Dreams. God's Forgotten Language.** 223p. notes. Crossroad Publishing Co. N.Y., 1984.

The relationship of dreams to religious experience in a book designed for the general reader. The author stresses ordinary rather than complex dreams, and explains what their religious aspects have to say on the relationship between "evil and the divine." Sanford writes that he is not concerned in this writing with a theological God, but to dreams from God that "revolve around a central authority in the psyche." The creative element in all dreams, he believes, is in itself divine, and carries God's message to man.

Sanford's ideas blend Jungian and Christian concepts in measures acceptable to both. The book was originally published in Zurich in 1968, by the C.G. Jung Institute under the title, Gottes vergessene Sprache.

**Saul (Leon J.). Technic and Practice of Psychoanalysis.** 244p. index. J.B. Lippincott. Philadelphia, 1958.

Psychoanalytic handbook for students written by a professor of clinical psychiatry at the University of Pennsylvania Medical School. This is a standard Freudian approach in which Saul begins with the statement that "The interpretation of dreams is a cornerstone of the psychoanalytic technique." He reminds his reader that Freud did not begin with an interest in dreams but developed such interest only because his patients insisted on telling him their dreams, demanding that he give them an explanation.

Saul points out that during World War II, "nightmares were one of the constant symptoms of 'combat fatigue.'" In his section on working with dreams, Dr. Saul reports a dream, then provides data on the patient's associations, enabling the analyst to arrive at an interpretation. He is an advocate of the value of dreams in analysis, particularly as a method of dealing with a patient who shows little or no progress, or if the core of the dynamics, the nuclear emotional constellation, is difficult to understand. His approach: review the first ten dreams of the analysis, isolate these from the other material, and also review the current set of dreams. Saul ends his section on dream interpretation by cautioning the student that "It cannot be emphasized too strongly that for treatment, full associations to the dream elements must be obtained."

**Sauneron (Serge, et al.). Les Songes et leur interprétation.** (Sources Orientales II) 331p. notes, maps, biblios, index. Ed. Du Seuil. Paris, 1959.

An attempt by twelve orientalists to present papers on dreams and dream interpretation in ancient Egypt, Babylonia, among the Hittites, in Canaan and Israel, in traditional Islam, Persia, Kurdistan, India, among the Ural-Altaics, in Cambodia, China, and Japan.

Each scholar reviews the literature (primarily classical), contributes selected dreams, and, where possible, provides us with a brief comment on the sources and methods of dream interpretation. As expected, the results are mixed.

Professor Serge Sauneron's work on dreams in ancient

Egypt, Marcel Leibovici's work on Babylonia, Toufy Fahd's paper on dream interpretation in Islam, and Anne-Marie Esnoul's work on those in India are of value, each with references and its own bibliography.

In the other papers, one is led to believe that these societies did very little dreaming, or that the topic was not worthy of serious scholarly consideration, at least not in more than a dozen or so pages. Also one regrets that these papers reflected no concepts other than those of oriental scholars with no special knowledge of dreams or dream interpretation. Thus we lack evidence of anything like the cross-cultural brilliance found in the writings of Lincoln and others. In short, a good idea poorly done.

**Saurat (Denis). Death and the Dreamer.** 150p. illus. Westhouse. London, 1946.

The author's collected dreams which purport to relate back to earlier life, all triggered by a bomb exploding in London during World War II.

**Savary (Louis M. et al.). Dreams and Spiritual Growth: A Christian Approach to Dreamwork.** With More than 35 Dreamwork Techniques. 241p. notes, biblio. Paulist Press. N.Y., 1984.

Engaging dream workbook with a Christian orientation. The three authors, who include Patricia H. Berne and Strephon Kaplan Williams, as well as Savory, announce that they have written a primer "for using your dreams to connect you with God, yourself, and the believing community."

The book contains a rich body of historical data on the early Christian church's views of dreams and dreamwork. Many of the anecdotes are enlightening. We learn, for example, that Gregory the Great warned that only saints could ascertain the real meaning of dreams, while Ignatius Loyola instructed his Jesuits that "prayerwork" was the path to salvation. Loyola's prayerwork, in fact, seems not too far removed from the daydreaming techniques found in Jung's active imagination.

Following their historical introduction, the authors offer the reader a veritable panorama of dream techniques. The reader is taught how to keep a dream journal, and how to talk to a figure that appears in his dreams. Dream symbols are explained, as is the nature and meaning of the "waking" dream. One is instructed in the techniques for using dreams in healing, as well as the best way to form a group dream workshop.

The authors do their best to point out to Christians that recent discoveries in dream techniques are not fraught with occultism and witchcraft. While it may be difficult to walk (or dream) a direct path from Dreams and Spiritual Growth to God and Eternal Salvation, the authors' efforts should dampen any qualms voiced by ardent religious practitioners that modern dreamwork techniques are unchristian.

**Scherer (Friedrich). Das Walten von Wahrheit und Wahn.** 112p. Privately published by the author. Coburg, (1950?).

This monograph is purportedly devoted entirely to dreams of the blind, with emphasis on historical examples of dreams, derived primarily from European and Germanic literature.

**Scherner (Karl A.). Das Leben des Traums.** 656p. Berlin, 1861.

A landmark book, involving the first attempt at scientific dream interpretation in the modern sense. Dr. Scherner, a professor of philosophy at the University of Breslau, abandoned the prophetic interpretations of the more popular dream books, seeking apparently for the first time to uncover the psychological content which formed the heart of the dream. In so doing, Scherner tried to create a complete theory of dream symbolism. Dreams, he believed, were brought on by various body stimulations.

Scherner's book apparently suffered from a lack of interest for almost forty years, until his researches came to the attention of Sigmund Freud. In fact, so important was the earlier work of Scherner to Freud, that Max Serog, writing in his New Light on Dreams (p. 10) claims that "Most of the ideas of this book, its whole dream phenomenology, even its analysis of dreams" reappear in the writings of Freud. Sigmund Freud himself wrote in his The Interpretation of Dreams (p. 115) that Scherner's book included "the most original and far-reaching attempt to explain dreaming as a special activity of the mind, capable of free expansion only during the state of sleep . . . ."

**Schmitt (Abraham). Before I Wake. Listening to God in Your Dreams.** 160p. Abingdon Press. Nashville, 1984.

Psychologist and theologian offers ten steps for the Christian to discover his God through dreams. The book is simply written, and appears designed for use in a church instructional setting that would appeal especially to teenagers. Dreams are not seen as expressions of turmoil, conflict, or suppressed wishes, but primarily as messages, not from the body or the unconscious, but from God.

Before I Wake provides many examples of God speaking to the dreamer, and is, I suspect, one of the few books on dreams that would appeal to fundamentalist Christians. Seeming to ignore all serious work on dreams from Freud to REM, Schmitt turns back the clock to dreams as revelations, reminiscent more of the dawn of the Christian era than of the final years of the twentieth century.

**Schneider (David M.) & Sharp (Lauriston). The Dream Life of a Primitive People. The Dreams of the Yir Yoront of Australia.** 122p. American Anthropological Association Anthropological Studies. No. 1. Washington, D.C., 1969.

First publication of a 1941 study containing the dream life of an Australian aboriginal group of the western coasts of the Cape York Peninsula. Supplies verbatim accounts of dreams of sexual intercourse, aggression, death, and of whites and white culture.

The authors' critique probes the relationship between dreams and the Yir Yoront culture, particularly as expressed by the manifest content of the dreams. The approximately 150 dreams recorded (as reported by 51 different dreamers) were gathered by Lauriston Sharp between 1933 and 1935.

The Yir Yoront were not particularly interested in dreams, and did not see dreams as being sent by spirits, though they did believe that a dream could be sent by another person. The dream was also apparently little used for prognostication in this culture.

**Scholz (Friedrich). Sleep and Dreams. A Scientific-Popular Dissertation.** Translated by H.M. Jewett. 147p. Funk & Wagnalls Co. London/N.Y., 1893.

An important monograph by the Director of the Bremen Insane Asylum. The German original, Schlaf und Traum, was published in Leipzig in 1887. Scholz viewed dreams as more painful than pleasurable, containing a memory of experiences we had forgotten in our waking lives. Dreams, however, presented materials in allegorical rather than direct terms so that the truth in one's dream was seldom recognized.

"In dreams," Scholz wrote, "we learn to know ourselves as we are in spite of all the disguises we wear to the world . . . ." Sigmund Freud acknowledged the contributions of Scholz, and incorporated his concepts into the theories expounded in The Interpretation of Dreams.

**Schreiner (Olive). Dreams.** 163p. Little, Brown. Boston, 1902.

A novel, with little relevance to dream investigations. The author was an intimate of the psychologist, Havelock Ellis, and influenced by his writings on the role of sex in human behavior, which were published the same year as Freud's The Interpretation of Dreams.

**Schubert (Gotthilf Heinrich von). Die Symbolik des Traumes.** Faksimiledruck nach der Ausgabe von 1814. Mit einem Nachwort von Gerhard Sauder. 203;XXXIIp. Verlag Schneider. Heidelberg, 1968.

Romantic view of dreams as liberators of the spirit, freeing the soul from the bonds and restrictions of the senses. Schubert, a natural philosopher and dramatist, was much involved with myth and poetry, holding a mystical view of images and symbols, including those apparent in dreams. The language of symbols in dreams, to Schubert, differed from the speech and writing patterns that are consciously expressed, in that they are not learned, but spontaneous. Freud cited Schubert's inference that dream symbols could be considered a hieroglyphic form of speech, one given us by the unconscious.

Schubert, however, viewed these symbols as reflections of moral, rather than of psychic or emotional truths. To him, the message of the dream was ultimately spiritual, a guide to the teachings and ultimate truths of Christianity. Raymond Firth, in an analysis of Schubert's work, called it not only a Christian apologia, but "the most original of all the theoretical works consecrated to the Romantic myth of the Dream, because it 'looked into the inner world,' its author sought in himself the solution of the 'universal enigma.'"

**Schultz-Hencke (Harald). Lehrbuch der Traumanalyse.** 286p. notes, biblio. G. Thieme. Stuttgart, 1949.

Textbook attempt to expand on traditional Freudian dream interpretation, with some blending of depth psychology. The author argues that the dream is not an isolated structure, but should be considered only as it relates to the entire being. He sees dreams as manifestations of possessiveness, sexuality, or the drive for power.

**Schumann (Hans-Joachim von). Träume der Blinden. Vom Standpunkt der Phanomenologie, Tiefenpsychologie, Mythologie und Kunst.** 152p. notes, biblio. illus. [Psychologische Praxis, Heft 25] S. Karger. Basel, 1959.

Scholarly study of phenomenology, depth psychology, mythology, and art as manifested in the dreams of the blind. An important effort of research in the literature on this topic.

Dr. Schumann begins with a discussion of the medical fundamentals of blindness including those features which set the blind apart from sighted persons. He discusses dream interpretations of the blind from both the phenomenological and depth psychological approach.

The author examines the differences in dreams between those blind at birth, and those blinded later in life. There are examples of dreams of the blind from cultures ranging from Africa to Latin America, the nature of visual phenomena in dreams of the blind, the role of dreams of the blind in English drama and German romanticism, dreams of the blind in music, the dream in the Iliad and Odyssey, dreams of blind children, and the role of ESP in the blind, particularly in reference to dreams. The author also treats dreams of those blinded through brain injury.

After an extensive discussion of the psychology of the blinded person, Dr. Schumann follows with a discussion of the "soul of the blind," and concludes with a fascinating study of the nature of dreams by sighted people living in polar darkness, as in Greenland during the 24 hour periods of night. Dr. Schumann cites 239 different bibliographic sources in his investigations, and has done us a great service with the very thoroughness and carefulness of his research.

**Schuyler (Philippa and Josephine). Kingdom of Dreams.** 217p. illus., biblio. R.Speller & Sons. N.Y., 1966.

A popular presentation of dreams, with several interesting chapters seeking to trace man's spoken and written symbols to the possible source of their origin: man's unconscious. These symbols, argue the Schuylers, first appear in dreams, projecting themselves outward in the form of myths, numbers, words, emblems, signs, codes, "and formulas of all kinds with which we create the arts, philosophy, religion and science."

The authors provide us with a glossary of "permanent dream symbols" such as hawk (watchful, cruel), flowers (happiness, hope, spring) and rope (caught, to hang, justice). "The dream world which man inhabits is a complex of all his needs: food, safety, ambition, self-knowledge, procreation, sensation, aspiration," conclude the authors, "The problem of obtaining all of these is what occupies his dreams."

**Schwartz (Howard). Dream Journal, 1965–1974.** 40p. Tree Books. Berkeley, Calif., 1975.

Talented poet and writer's dream journal, including twenty dreams that survived the transition from sleeping to waking so well that Schwartz transformed them into short prose parables in a book. In his introduction, the author writes that he believes that dreams convey a message from (and serve as the tongue of) the unconscious to consciousness. He subscribes to the Fritz Perls' Gestaltist theory of taking the whole dream as projected parts of the dreamer, and role playing each of the parts oneself, including inanimate objects, describing this as the most useful view that he has encountered. Schwartz not only dreams, but can dream furiously. He reports, but, alas, does not recount on these pages, that he experienced no less than sixty dreams about a single girl.

The Dream Journal of Howard Schwartz is delightful reading in itself, and serves as but one more piece of raw material that may provide the investigator with a clue as to how the artist utilizes the stuff of dreams as an expression of his own creativity.

**Schwartzkopff (P.). Das Leben im Traum: Eine Studie.** Leipzig. 1887.

**Scott (Charles E., editor). On Dreaming. An Encounter with Medard Boss.** 118p. Scholars Press. Chico, Calif., 1977.

Includes a biography of Boss, a condensation of his major writing on dream analysis, followed by five professional critiques of his concepts and work. As a measure of the complexity of Boss' theories, it is not without reason that the principal critical comments on his observations are supplied by a group of philosopher-psychologists and theologians. See Boss' The Analysis of Dreams, in this bibliography.

**Scott (W. Clifford). Remembering Sleep and Dreams.** pp. 253-354. notes, biblio. [The International Review of Psycho-Analysis] Volume II, No. 3. N.Y., 1975.

This book-sized edition is devoted entirely to the writings of this noted Canadian psychoanalyst. The writings span thirty years of work related largely to problems of sleep and dreaming. The work of Dr. Scott is particularly valuable as an eloquent and sometimes highly persuasive defense for holding to the traditional dream theories of Freud against the revisions of many of his fellow analysts, as well as against the experimental neurologists, physiologists, and psychologists.

Dr. Scott chastizes his colleagues in a series of reviews of books and professional papers suggesting revisions in Freudian dream theories. He joins battle once again in his support of the Freudian position in light of the REM discoveries as of 1969. He defends with equal vigor both the dream as the guardian of sleep and the dream interpreted as the royal road to the unconscious.

Remembering Sleep and Dreams is written in a simple, concise prose style, although there are admittedly problems with continuity due to the disparity in subject matter. It is also disquieting to find neither table of contents, nor an index. Still, the matter discussed is of such importance that it should be consulted by all concerned with the future of psychoanalysis.

**Sechrist (Elsie). Dreams: Your Magic Mirror.** 212p. index. Cowles, N.Y., 1968.

This popular explanation of dreams and their meaning was issued by the Edgar Cayce Institute. Because of its many printings, this book received wide circulation and has influenced many nonprofessional readers. The author bases her interpretations largely on the work of the psychic Edgar Cayce. Included are simple, well written instructions for dream interpretation. Strong religious orientation.

**Sedir (Paul). Les Rêves.** M. Chacornac de Chameul. Paris, 1910.

The author wrote books on clairvoyance, spiritualism, and the Rosicrucian religion. I have been unable to locate a copy of this book.

**Serog (Max). New Light on Dreams. A New Approach to the Dream Problem.** 159p. biblio. House of Edinboro. Boston, 1953.

Interesting presentation of dreams and a theory of dream interpretation based upon forty-odd years of practice as a psychoanalyst. This is no Freudian interpretation. In fact Serog questions not only Freud's theories but the value of many tenets of psychoanalysis, and the concept of the unconscious as well. In this respect, it might be worthwhile to examine some of the author's arguments.

Dr. Serog's experience with dream therapy has led him to conclude that the dream is a state of primitive thought in which a visual hallucinatory experience takes place. The primitive thinking in the dream state is the same kind of thinking found in primitive tribes, in small children, in schizophrenics, and in creative art. Just as rational, logical thinking has become the basis of science and technique, so primitive thinking has become the hallmark of the dream.

In dream thinking the difference between image and reality blurs, as in wish and wish fulfillment, so that in dream thinking, wishes are easily fulfilled. On the other hand, Dr. Serog affirms that primitive thinking is the root of all creative and productive faculties, the source of artistic creation. But in the dream that thinking cannot accomplish creative work as it lacks intentional coordinated thinking, largely because the dream state is one of mental disintegration with the absence of increased mental abilities.

The author finds that prophetic dreams are more psychological than factual and "rest in the last analysis, upon the interlacing of fate and personality." Furthermore, there is no symbolism in dreams, since symbols are the product of logical, intentional, coordinated thinking. "In the dream," he concludes, "there is only the dream picture itself, and the immediate surrendering to the present impression, but there is no meaning or idea behind this impression."

While still acknowledging the value of dream interpretation, Dr. Serog cautions that it cannot be approached by logical rules, nor can it be tested. The interpretation of a specific dream is neither right nor wrong; it is either adequate or less adequate. Such interpretations cannot be tested, since they essentially consist of the immediate interpretation of emotional totality.

To the psychotherapist, there are no parts to a dream, rather it is "an immediate total emotional experience." He sees the dream as having particular value to the psychotherapist in depicting the changing attitude of the patient and, over the course of analysis, the progress shown as a result of the psychotherapeutic procedure.

New Light on Dreams received some very critical reviews. I particularly have in mind a review written by Dr. Max Friedemann, which appeared in one of the professional journals. Friedemann accused Serog of revitalizing old theories such as those of "dissociation and disintegration," which he hardly finds adequate substitutes for the dream theories of Freud. Nonetheless, Dr. Serog's book is stimulating and, despite its limitations, deserves consideration by the serious student of dreams.

**Servadio (Emilio). Il Sogno.** 95p. notes. A. Garzanti. Milano, 1955.

Traditional Freudian theory of dreams augmented by an interesting chapter on the possible role of telepathy in dreams, and another on the dream in folklore. Included is a brief examination of the dream theories of Stekel, Adler, and Jung.

**Sharma (Jagdish P.) & Siegel (Lee). Dream-Symbolism in the Sramanic Tradition. Two Psycholoanalytical Studies in Jinist & Buddhist Dream Legends.** 94p. illus., notes. Firma KLM Private Ltd. Calcutta, 1980.

Two separate studies carried out independently. Dr. Jagdish P. Sharma's "Symbolism in the Jinist Dream World," attempts a Jungian treatment of Jinist dream symbolism, based primarily on the Trisasti, a twelfth century Jinist treatise on religion and mythology. The Indian Jinists were much concerned with the dream world, and their traditions in this area date back 2,000 years. The author discusses the dreams that mothers of Jinist heros see at the time of conception, the myth of the transfer of the embryo, invented dreams, dreams of God's messages, and the symbol of the snake, monkey, holy fig tree, lion, and moon. Also included is an analysis of fourteen "great dreams," accompanied by the author's Jungian interpretations.

Dr. Lee Siegel's, "Out of the Palace of Pleasure," contributes a Freudian analysis of the biographical legends of the Buddha. He views the attainment of Buddhahood (nirvana), as a clear and complete resolution of the Oedipus complex, with its inward fulfillment and complete inward solution. Freud's view of our ontological predicament expressed in our psychological condition was, to Dr. Siegel, similar in many ways to that held by the Buddha. The suffering in Buddhism is paralleled in the pain of repression to be found in psychoanalytic theory.

In spite of many points in common, Dr. Siegel finds a basic difference in values and attitudes between Freud and the Buddha. Where Freud sought to endure the world and the self, the Buddha renounced the world and the self. Similarly, the liberation of the Buddha is from feeling, from the tragic; whereas the liberation of Oedipus is in feeling, in the tragic. For Freud and the Buddha this liberation is an arduous struggle, "the achievement of a 'hero' who confronts himself, all of himself." There is no confrontation more difficult, and none more important.

**Sharp (Daryl). The Secret Raven. Conflict and Transformation in the Life of Franz Kafka.** 128p. notes, index. Inner City Books. Toronto, 1980.

This Jungian analysis of the life and personality of Franz Kafka concentrates on his writing as a product of his life, rather than on the writings themselves. Sharp employs an analysis of Kafka's dreams as a guide to Kafka's inner conflicts, centering on his intense feelings for his mother, and offset by the rages and fears of a child abandoned.

**Sharpe (Ella F.). Dream Analysis. A Practical Handbook for Psycho-Analysts.** 211p. notes, index. Hogarth Press. London, 1949.

First printing of a series of lectures on dreams given by the author to students at the Institute of Psycho-Analysis in London during the years 1934 and 1936. Dr. Sharpe argues brilliantly for a continuation of extensive dream analysis in therapy at a time when some analysts were considering turning to the concept of transference/countertransference as an equal, if not more important, method of therapy than dream inpretation. With her emphasis on dreams, Dr. Sharpe adroitly puts theory into practice, perceiving dreams as unifying the past and the present.

There are many examples of dreams drawn from the author's clinical practice, illustrating the dream as a typical and individual psychical product, the mechanisms of dream formation, and the evaluation of dreams in psychoanalytic practice. Dr. Sharpe approaches dreams with a vitality and originality seldom encountered in this type of pedantic presentation. There is a certain beauty in her writing unexpected in a psychoanalytic treatise. Add to this a very useful index of specific dreams, accompanied by the author's own content analysis of individual dreams.

**Sherwood (Jane). The Fourfold Vision. A Study of**

**Consciousness, Sleep and Dreams.** 222p. index. Neville Spearman, Ltd. London, 1965.

Medium's theory of consciousness based on four levels of being: physical, etheric, astral, and the ego. In a vivid dream of a mother having her baby fall from her arms into a river, the chain of events, according to Sherwood's theory is as follows: (1) stimulation of the aural nerve when a few drops of rain fell upon the dreamer (physical cause); (2) interpretation as sensation (etheric cause); (3) recall of the astral (feeling of alarm); and, (4) the recall of the ego (supplying a hurried meaning to the context of the emotional and sensation situation).

Sherwood believes that the dream time might last as long as it would in normal activity, except that dreams "are smoothed out by the [absence] of the necessity of interaction." She also argues against Freudian interpretations of symbols in dreams, particularly those suggesting a sexual repression. The author sees dreams as being but a part of the great "astral body," helping nourish it in preparation for one's next existence, "for what is left of the man when his earth-body falls away from him?"

Recommended only for those with free flowing psyches whose tastes in dreamwork do not require that their feet touch ground.

**Shohet (Robin). Dream Sharing. How to Enhance Your Understanding of Dreams by Group Sharing and Discussion.** 176p. notes, index. Turnstone Press. Wellingborough, England, 1985.

Experiences and successful techniques employed by a marital therapist with eight years of experience in group dreamwork. Shohet stresses the value of group dreamwork in familiar and related settings, as well as in groups of interested strangers. She believes group dream therapy can be of great value in resolving family problems and within a school setting.

Robin Shohet has contributed an easily read and informative book that explains the techniques and benefits to be derived from group dreamwork, with many helpful examples, and with a chapter on beginning one's own dream group.

**Shulman (Sandra). Nightmare.** 244p. illus., biblio., index. Macmillan. N.Y., 1979.

Nontechnical exposition of the nightmare. Includes a review of the impact of the nightmare on the lives of notable figures of the past, the significance of the nightmare on personal development and in mental disease, and the so-called prophetic nightmare. The book ends with a discussion of modern psychiatric theories as to its causes and cure. This work is an expansion on the author's earlier monograph, Dreams: The Interpretation of Dreams and Nightmares. A Modern Survey, published in 1970.

**Shuttle (Penelope) & Redgrove (Peter). The Wise Wound. Menstruation and Everywoman.** 335p. notes. index. V. Gollancz. London, 1978.

An important and illuminating book, authored by a poet and a novelist, writing as "equal and complementary partners." This work seeks to ease both pain and depression in the woman undergoing her menstrual cycle through the analysis of dreams occurring during this period. The orientation is largely Jungian, particularly the authors' examination of dreams during menstruation, reflecting the spiritual animus guide.

Shuttle and Redgrove ply us with a wealth of anthropological and mythological support in their effort to demonstrate that a woman's suffering during this period results more from her failure to recognize and adapt to her psychic/physical life cycle than to the physiological process alone. An excellent study in a much neglected area. The Wise Wound should be read by every analytical therapist.

**Silberer (Herbert). Der Traum. Einführung in die Traumpsychologie.** 123p. notes, biblio. Bonset. Amsterdam, 1966.

Silberer's brief monograph was originally published in 1919. It makes an important contribution to dream theory. In an expansion upon the theories of Freud, Silberer developed a theory of the functional phenomena of dreams. Dreams show the way the psyche functions as differentiated from mental and bodily activity. These functional moments in the dream are revealed by a subjective feeling tone or emotion, and can be characterized by attraction, repulsion, ease, effort, laziness, perseverance, increase, decrease, or change. Dreams are therefore mirrors of the psyche and may serve several purposes. Dreams may integrate external impressions which we perceive only instinctually and reveal them with bold certainty in the dream. They may reveal the true essence of the dreamer. And dreams may offer presentiment of an approaching illness during the incubation of the infection where "it is heard only as if through a microphone or seen through a microscope, thanks to the exaggerating qualities of the dream."

In this context, Silberer anticipated by many decades modern dream theories. Indeed, his contribution was acknowledged by Freud himself, when in his Introduction of Narcissism, Freud referred to Silberer's functional phenomena concept as "one of the few supplements to the dream theory, the value of which is indisputable." In his opening paragraph to this book, Silberer writes, "The mysterious, the enigmatic, have always had an attraction for the human mind, especially the enigma of the human soul." Silberer's search required that he pursue that quest in man's dreams. And in this, it seems, lies the real purpose of all those who toil in these vineyards.

**Simon (P.M.). Le Monde des rêves.** 213p. Alcon. Paris, 1888.

Simon speculated on the role of dreams as premonitions of physical and mental illness. He was particularly interested in dreams manifesting fear and anxiety, as well as in nightmares. Simon believed that various stimuli would affect dreams. Specific organs, if diseased or inflamed, would probably be reflected in the patient's dreams. He cites certain wish fulfillment dreams, particularly the hunger dreams of Baron Trenck while being held prisoner. Freud acknowledged Simon's contribution to his theories.

**Simpson (David). A Discourse on Dreams and Night-Visions With Numerous Examples Ancient and Modern.** 134p. Printed by Edward Bayley. London, 1791.

Speculations of an English clergyman on the nature of dreams. Simpson believed that dreams played a major role in the affairs of men throughout the world. They are, he argued "of equal authority with the Bible." The author later amplified these views to suggest that both dreams and night visions acted more powerfully upon the minds of man "than the most pure and refined concepts." Mr. Simpson provides the reader with examples of important and significant dreams of celebrated individuals from the Biblical era to the 18th century.

**Singer (June). Boundaries of the Soul. The Practice of Jungian Psychology.** 479p. biblio., index. Doubleday. Garden City, N.Y., 1973.

Valuable introduction to Jungian dream interpretation in the practice of psychotherapy. Contains two exciting chapters on the understanding of dreams and Jung's theory of dreams in active imagination.

**Sleep and Dream Research.** Published by the Research and Education Assoc. 374p. tables, biblio. N.Y., 1982.

Reports of research and laboratory studies in a compilation supported financially by the National Institute of Mental Health. This survey has the appearance of a rush government contract report, and is not helped by poor organization, the absence of annotations, and no index. There are two sections on dreams: The dream state of REM, and a chapter on the meaning of dreams, which consists of an eighteen page summary of research. It is small wonder no writer puts his name to this work. The public should demand its tax money back.

**Sloane (Paul). Psychoanalytic Understanding of the Dream.** 373p. biblio., index. J. Aronson. N.Y., 1979.

A very good handbook on the technique of dream analysis designed to acquaint the psychoanalytic student with the art of dream interpretation. Dr. Sloane, while conducting his own seminars, concluded that many of his analytic candidates were "largely at sea when they came to deal with dreams," in spite of the importance for the psychoanalyst of making the latent meaning of the dream available both to himself as well as to the patient.

This book is a product of the specialized course developed by Dr. Sloane in dream analysis. It certainly does its job. Emphasizing what might be termed "the case-study method," Dr. Sloane covers the manifest dream, the dream wish, early dreams and premature interpretations, transference dreams, resistance and dreams, dreams with unpleasurable affects, validation of interpretation and terminal dreams, that is those demonstrating the end of analysis. In each chapter cases are presented, giving the patient's background, the day residue, the dream itself, and a discussion centering upon possible interpretations.

The orientation is neo-Freudian, of course, and Dr. Sloane points out that most of the dreams reported are those of patients with well-integrated and intact egos, although most "suffered for the most part from unconscious conflicts which had persisted since childhood." All in all, a solid contribution in which the author has done what he set out to do.

**Smith (Elizabeth Oakes). Shadow Land: Or, The Seer.** 129p. Fowlers and Wells. N.Y., 1852.

Semi-autobiographical account of the occult experiences of a widely read feminist author of the middle of the last century. Elizabeth Smith's strong Christian beliefs played a major role in her parapsychological experiences, and she attributes many of her dream experiences to "the spiritual essences." Dreams, she believed, always had their origin "from some subject connected with our previous thoughts." Although sleep, releasing one from the clogged external world, is "more spiritualized in nature, . . . a disenthralment of the soul, leaving it to a joyous freedom of condition."

Smith recounts many of her more interesting dreams in this writing, cautioning the reader that, in her dreams at least, one did not dream of close ones or of those in whom we are most interested, but the "spirit guides us from exhausted ideas to a new subject." Similarly, she did not dream of the death of friends, "as though the spiritual vision associated with them were already overdone . . . ."

Most interesting are Ms. Smith's experiences with lucid dreaming (pp. 107-108), which she called double dreaming. "Not unfrequently," she writes, "we not only dream, but dream we are telling our dream." Once, dreaming of a high marble room with windows in deep embrasures, lofty in height, and abundant in tracery, she thought, all is foreign to me, and said in her sleep, "Oh, I am in Italy again." Many times, she recalls, "I dream that I am dreaming."

An interesting personalized and well-told, if not scientific, early memoir on the value of dreams and the experiences of an early feminist dreamer.

**Smith (Howard E. Jr.). Dreams in Your Life.** 173p. illus. index. Doubleday. Garden City, N.Y., 1975.

Professional science writer's excellent introductory book for older children. Includes well written and illustrated text, with simple prose explanations of the occult, early dream interpretation, dream laboratories, ESP, nightmares, and understanding dreams.

**Sneed (J.W.). Jean Paul's "Dreams."** 111p. notes, index. Oxford University Press. N.Y., 1966.

Scholarly examination of dream-visions in European history and culture. An emphasis is given the dreams of Jean Paul Richter (1763-1825), a visionary and mystic. The approach is historical rather than psychological, and there is no attempt at a Freudian or Jungian interpretation. An appendix contains selected examples of celebrated visionary dreams drawn from German history.

**Solotareff (Jeanine). Le Symbolisme dans les rêves. La Méthode de traduction de Paul Diel.** 362p. Payot. Paris, 1979.

Paul Diel (1893-1972) was a French psychiatrist and author, primarily concerned with symbolism. He practiced for many years at the Laboratoire de Psychobiologie de l'enfant. Diel's writings show the influence of both Freud and Jung, and to a lesser extent, that of Adler. He viewed the dream as a product of the human psyche, evolving from the imagination and showing the universal truths of mythic symbolism.

Dr. Solotareff has drawn upon Diel's manuscripts and diaries in the preparation of this book, presenting Diel's concepts of the symbolic expression of the language of dreams, accompanied by twenty-seven recorded dreams, along with Dr. Diel's explanation of their meaning. The final dream examined is that of Descartes.

**Sonnet (Andre). The Twilight Zone of Dreams.** Translated from the German by J. Thomas Fraser. 230p. biblio., index. Chilton Co. Phila., 1961.

Well-documented book of research into literature (biographies, memoirs, philosophical inquiries, etc.) in which various authors touched the parapsychological aspects of dreaming: telepathy and clairvoyance in dreams, creative accomplishments in dreams, premonitions of death in dreams, warnings and hunches in dreams, and the dream as a bridge to the subconscious. Sonnet cites many European intellectuals, scientists, and authors of the 18th, 19th, and early 20th centuries, suggesting ample literary if nonexperimental evidence of extrasensory phenomena in dreams.

This is a translation of the author's Die Rätselhafte Welt der Traume, originally published in 1959. Unfortunately the only laboratory evidence cited by Sonnet consists largely of Rhine's research, and the translator or publisher seems to have eliminated the lengthy bibliography of sources cited in the main body of research. Still, this book should not be overlooked by those interested not so much in dreams as tools of therapy as in dreams as a reflection of the twilight zone of the psyche.

**Southey (Robert). The Correspondence of Robert Southey and Caroline Bowles, to Which are Added: Correspondence with Shelley, and Southey's Dreams.** Edited, with an introduction by Edward Dowden. 388p. Port. Dublin Univ. Press. Dublin, 1881.

While preparing the letters of Southey and Bowles for publication, Edward Dowden, came by chance across a collection of Southey's dreams, which Southey called his "register of some fantastic dreams." These dreams are included as an appendix to this volume (pp. 366-384) and consist of thirty-nine dreams recorded between 1804 and 1832. Most are given without comment, but a few contain Southey's interpretations.

The dreams themselves, ranging from nightmare qualities to vivid tales of the supernatural, make for a unique contribution to the psychology of this genius poet. The editor laments that Shelley too had considered such a collection of his own dreams, and had tentatively titled the work, Catalogue of the Phenomena of Dreams, As Connecting Sleeping and Waking. But the nature of Shelley's dreams apparently dissuaded him. "Here," he reported, "I was obliged to leave off, overcome by thrilling horror."

Of course not all great writers could call upon their dreams as vehicles for literary inspiration. Recall the lament of Charles Lamb when he anquished, "The poverty of my dreams mortifies me. There is Coleridge, at his will can conjure up icy domes, and pleasure-houses of Kubla Khan, and Abyssinian maids, and songs of Abora, and caverns . . . to solace his night solitudes, when I cannot muster a fiddle . . . ." (Witches and Other Night Fears).

**Sparrow (Gregory S.). Lucid Dreaming. Dawning of the Clear Light.** Revised edition. 69p. biblio. A.R.E. Press. Virginia Beach, Virginia, 1976.

Lucid dreaming techniques based on the Edgar Cayce philosophy. While Cayce does not mention this method, the author points out that he would have approved of lucid dreaming as a means of physically leaving one's present circumstances in the body and world in order to achieve a "self-reflecting consciousness." Sparrow has conducted successful courses on lucid dreaming at the Association for Research and Enlightenment, which stresses physical and spiritual betterment through many techniques, not the least of which is dreamwork.

The beginner in lucid dreaming, particularly those who have had no success, will want to consult this slim handbook before admitting defeat. More than one novice has achieved lucid dreaming by following Sparrow's advice after failing with other, more widely known, handbooks.

**Speck (Frank G.). Naskapi. The Savage Hunters of the Labrador Peninsula.** 248p. illus., map, notes, glossary, index. University of Oklahoma Press. Norman, 1935.

The Naskapi consider the dream a religious process and a part of the larger process of revelation by which the individual acquires a knowledge of life. Naskapi also follow messages given in their dreams, regardless of the consequences. All other considerations are subordinated to the fulfillment of the dream.

Communication with the "unseen world" is accomplished through the dream, specifically by talking to the "soul spirit," who provides the dreamer with direction and guidance in life. The Naskapi consider frequent dreams a blessing. They fast, dance, sing, take sweat baths, meditate, eat large amounts of meat, and even drink animal grease to induce dreaming. There is no evidence that the Naskapi attempt to control or influence the content of their dreams.

Dream interpretation is accomplished by casting the bones of slain animals as a guide to divination. This technique plays other roles in the religion and culture of these people as well. The most common result of dream messages seems to relate to survival, particularly to hunting. Speck's book contains sketches and narrative examples of Naskapi undertaking beaver and caribou hunts as a result of messages given by their soul spirit in dreams.

Dreams received and interpreted had to be paid for. Payment is made to the spirits of the animals killed in the hunt, as well as to the source of the dreams themselves. One form of payment consists of post-mortem rites centering on the bones of the animals killed. Another relates to art. Symbolic and decorative art in the form of drawings, hand rattles, and drums are dedicated to animals killed and to dream spirits. Indeed, there appears to exist a very close relationship between art and the dream in Naskapi society.

The author believes that Naskapi dream beliefs parallel closely those of the Huron Indians of earlier years, and cites early Jesuit relations depicting similar practices in the early seventeenth century. This evidence is important, since it demonstrates the role of dreams in these societies in their natural state before coming under the influence of the white man.

**Spier (Leslie). Yuman Tribes of the Gila River.** 345p. Univ. of Chicago Press. Chicago, 1933.

In the Yuman Maricopa tribes of North America the basis of religion, according to Spier (p. 186), was dream experience with spirit birds and animals.

**Spiller (G.). A Contribution Towards A Science of Dreams.** 16p. The Farleigh Press. London, 1934.

One is amazed at the breadth of dream concepts covered in this brief monograph. Dr. Spiller, author of The Mind of Man and other books on human psychology, presents here a paper representing "two years of systematic daily dream observations." Among his observations, the author discusses lucid dreaming (which he calls the semi-consciousness of dreaming); the possibility that he has had dreams which last for hours; his dreams which have had color, light, sound, touch, and smell; passing from one dream to another; stock dreams (for him: flying, running quickly, etc.); exaggeration in dreams; memory and imagination in dreams; and, dream causes.

Spiller concludes that "our dream knowledge and our dream character roughly reflect our waking knowledge and our waking character." He believed that dreams are caused by physical stimuli, such as cold and heat, loud sounds, glaring lights. "The serious problems of life and current events," he suggests, "leave dream life almost entirely unaffected." As for the function of dreams, the author points to "the utter hopelessness of the view that there is a rigid connection between dreams and unfulfilled waking desires." As for dream symbolism, Spiller writes, "In two years' daily observations of dreams, I have not noticed a single symbolical dream and much doubt their existence except as a great rarity."

**Spitta (H.). Die Schlaf- und Traumzustande der menschlichen Seele.** 376p. notes. Tubingen, 1878.

Spitta wrote that dreams were due either to nervous stimulation or to association. He found the solution to a dream problem centered on identifying the proper relationship between the somatic sources of the dream and its ideational content. One of the questions in diagnosis, Spitta found, was that the order and coherence given to the dream by the patient was a result of conscious reorganization of the dream content by the patient after awakening. Spitta found that subjective feelings and longings are most likely to reveal themselves during the dream state, usually as a method of dramatizing an idea or emotion. Spitta was a major contributor to Freud in the development of his theories. Freud cited this author seventeen times in his The Interpretation of Dreams. This work was reprinted in 1882, but has never been translated into English.

**Sri Aurobindo. The Works of Sri Aurobindo.** 30 volumes.

Aurobindo Birth Centenary Library. Pondicherry, India. 1970-1975.

Sri Aurobindo (1872-1950) was one of the foremost yoga philosophers in modern India. His teachings have exerted a great influence on Tantra and other schools of present-day yoga. Sri Aurobindo writes that the dream is a temporary state that replaces the infinite. The level of dream-consciousness is experienced as equal to a "pure and featureless self-aware Existence." This philosopher sees the task of the individual in yoga as experiencing and enhancing ever-ascending levels of dreams until he or she reaches the highest level: that of the subliminal, or supra-consciousness. These ever-higher levels in dreams are attained through lucid and controlled dreaming.

Sri Aurobindo's principal writings on the significance and role of the dream in yoga appear in two volumes of this collection, The Life Divine (vol. 18) and Letters on Yoga (vol. 24). His methods of working with the dream are intertwined closely with the complexities of yoga, and are definitely not recommended to those unwilling to undergo a long period of study and practice.

**Staff (Vera S.). Remembered on Waking. Concerning Psychic and Spiritual Dreams and Theories of Dreaming.** 149p. [Mysticism Committee, Churches' Fellowship for Psychical and Spiritual Studies] Crowborough, Sussex, England, 1975.

A review of the literature and reports on dreams portending future events. The author begins with a summary of these dreams as they appeared in the Bible, followed by a survey of precognitive dreams in historical literature. The most interesting section concerns a project undertaken by the Churches' Fellowship for Psychical and Spiritual Studies in this area. The project was advertised in the CFPSS Quarterly Review, and sixty-five individuals responded by questionnaire.

According to Staff, fifty-eight of the respondents were women, primarily middle-aged or elderly. She reports on a total of forty psychic dreams, although she does not state whether these were multiple dreams reported by a few dreamers or primarily one for each dreamer. The author concludes that these dreams varied from the most trivial to those predicting a public event.

Staff presents interesting examples of many of the dreams sent to her organization, but makes no attempt at serious quantitative classification. She stresses that psychic dreaming represents messages from the soul which put the dreamer in touch with God.

**Starker (Steven). Fantastic Thought. All About Dreams, Daydreams, Hallucinations, and Hypnosis.** 164;6p. biblio. Prentice-Hall. Englewood Cliffs, N.J., 1982.

Professor of medical psychology seeks to integrate the concept of individual "fantasy styles" in the various altered states of consciousness into a practical tool which the individual can utilize to better his or her own life. Dr. Starker begins with a nontechnical examination of dreams and fantasies, reviews recent research, and suggests applications both in the fields of psychotherapy and mental health. In his sections on "fantastic therapy," the author touches on guided daydreams, their modification in oneirotherapy, and closes with a holistic method designed to promote better mental and physical health.

Unfortunately, for those interested in the dream, emphasis in this work is given to conscious waking or daydream methodologies. In spite of the well-formulated coverage in this area, one will search in vain for an extensive discussion of dreamwork as a tool in this holistic process.

**Steele (Marion A.) and Armstrong (Ronald M.). "I Had the Craziest Dream Last Night." A Psychiatrist Helps You Interpret Your Dreams.** 238p. Nelson-Hall Company. Chicago, 1971.

Dr. Steele, a psychiatrist, teams with a free lance writer in an effort to explain dreams to the uninitiated layman. If there was a contest of wills, the free lance writer clearly won. Serious discussion dims before a cute, overly simplistic formula heavily spiced throughout with sex.

**Stein (Murray, editor). Jungian Analysis.** Introduction by June Singer. 409p. bibliographies, index. Shambhala, Colorado, 1984.

Nineteen papers on the theory and application of Jungian analysis written for psychotherapists. James A. Hall, a clinical professor of psychiatry at the University of Texas, contributes the one chapter on the use of dreams and dream interpretation in analysis, though examples of dreams appear in many of these papers. Dr. Edith Sullwold discusses dream therapy in her excellent paper on the treatment of children, while Jungian dream theory and methodology appear in equally important writings by Katherine Bradway, Donald F. Sandner and John Beebe, and Edward C. Whitmont.

In his stimulating chapter on dream interpretation, Dr. Hall effectively argues that Jungian analysts should encourage their analysands to record their dreams. He is concerned about the "peculiar danger" in Jungian analysis of what he calls archetypal reductionism, the type of error which he believes was made by Freud when he discovered only a few core meanings, "invariably sexual," in a whole universe of images.

He also warns against another form of interpersonal reductionism found by "invariably referring all dreams to the transference-countertransference relationship between the analysand and the analyst." Hall suggests this process may strengthen a transference neurosis as well as cause both the analyst and analysand to miss the materials being produced by the unconscious.

Dr. Sullwold, founding Director of the Hilde Kirsch Children's Center, C.G. Jung Institute of Los Angeles, maintains a private practice for children. She offers a theoretical framework and practical techniques for approaching the child's inner world: painting, drawing sand play, and puppetry. These methods can also be used to explore the contents of dreams, which are the voice of that inner life. Dr. Sullwold describes the power of the child's images. If the contents of the dream, the images, are explored for meaning through any of these mediums, then that image can be integrated into life. Above all, Dr. Sullwold insists, one must honor the dream. The author's respect, acceptance, and love of children pervades this paper.

In "Psychopathology and Analysis," Donald F. Sandner and John Beebe, both Jungian analysts, offer an impressive, examination of neurotic conditions and psychopathology as revealed through dreams. They begin with Jung's discovery that dreams show complexes moving and interacting, often as pairs of opposites. Through numerous dream examples, the authors describe weakened ego states, various complexes, and the psyche's urge towards self-realization.

**Steiner (Rudolf). Knowledge of the Higher Worlds and**

**Its Attainment.** 224p. Anthroposophic Press. Spring Valley, N.Y., 1947.

Well-known work by the noted German occultist and mystic. In one chapter on dreams, Steiner advises that one's dreams change as he reaches a higher stage of psychic development, allowing the dreamer to enter a world beyond his senses. Steiner suggests a form of dream incubation to "raise to a higher ego," reaching for a "higher consciousness." Dreams, Steiner concludes, allow for one's entry into the astral world.

**Stekel (Wilhelm). Die Sprache des Traumes.** 320p. notes, biblio. J.F. Bergmann. Wiesbaden, 1911.

As with his celebrated contemporaries (Jung, Adler, and Rank), Wilhelm Stekel began as a student of and collaborator with Freud, only to break away eventually to found his own school of psychoanalysis. This work is a textbook in Freudian dream theory, detailing with amazing clarity the latent and manifest content of 594 individual dreams.

These dreams are classified by subject. There are sections on death and number symbolism, stereotyped dreams, artificial, and telepathic dreams. The author also discusses at great length the varying ways that masturbation may appear in dreams.

Yet even at this early stage, Stekel did not always adhere to Freudian theory, particularly in his examination of the concepts stressing the possible bipolarity of all psychic phenomena, i.e., that all sexual symbols are originally bisexual, and that bisexuality plays an important role in all neurotic behavior. An English translation, titled The Language of Dreams, was published in Boston by Richard G. Badger in 1922.

**Stekel (Wilhelm). Die Träume der Dichter.** 252p. J.F. Bergmann. Wiesbaden, 1912.

Wilhelm Stekel was a gifted musician, composer, playwright, and poet, as well as a psychoanalyst. Perhaps these interests led him to draw a comparison between poets, neurotics, and criminals. Before writing this book, Stekel prepared a detailed questionnaire on dreams which he sent to over fifty creative writers, basing much of this work on their written responses.

Stekel found that "the common factor in all three [poets, neurotics, and criminals] was a strong development of inherited instincts, a throwback, or atavism." All minds, Stekel argues, contain bipolar tendencies "directed toward both destruction and construction." But where the poet finds constructive expression through his creative effort, the criminal, lacking such an outlet, is overcome by his destructive impulses which he expresses through crime and violence. "In many dreams of poets I was able to prove that unconsciously they were discharging criminal impulses," concludes Stekel.

Die Träume der Dichter examines this bipolarization in the dreams of poets, playwrights, and authors. Stekel's analysis of the dreams of Josef Popper, Gerhart Hauptmann, and many others was conducted only after reviewing these creative writers' written responses. His studies of others, like Flaubert and Ibsen, were conducted primarily by a review of their autobiographical materials and printed works. Stekel closes his book with a detailed analysis of the dreams of the Austrian poet and dramatist, Friedrich Hebbel, suggesting religious, oedipal, homosexual, and criminal themes.

Die Träume der Dichter was Stekel's favorite book. It received excellent reviews, but sold poorly. Perhaps this is why it has never been translated into English.

**Stekel (Wilhelm). Der telepathische Traum. Meine Erfahrungen über die Phanomene des Hellsehens im Wachen und im Träume.** 112p. Wendepunkt-Verlag. Zurich/Leipzig, 1927.

Stekel, in this brief monograph, argues that the proof of telepathic dreams "is indisputable." He cites several cases from his own experience, including a case where husband and wife, both patients of his, had the same dream, even though neither confided in the other. Stekel also reflects Adlerian themes in his view of telepathic dreams, suggesting that dreams are the explorers of the future, and it is through these dream explorations that the analyst uncovers the patient's attitudes, methods, and ways of life.

**Stekel (Wilhelm). Fortschritte und Technik der Traumdeutung.** 450p. notes, biblio. index. Weidman. Vienna, 1935.

Stekel's major effort is essentially an enlargement of many Freudian postulates into a dream theory which he termed "active analysis." Stekel's later concepts were influenced both by his work as a military analyst treating cases of "shell shock" during World War I, as well as by the writings of Alfred Adler. Stekel believed that neurosis (which he termed parapathy) was brought on by the conflict between impulse and inhibition no less than by repressed sexuality. Certain disturbed patients, he writes, exhibit both moral as well as sexual repressions.

To Stekel, the nature of the dream is a product of the nature of repression. Thus the author recommends an advance in dream interpretation from the passive methods of free association recommended by Freud, to an active interpretation (active analysis) in which more stress is given to the manifest content of the dream, and less to the "artificialized and forced explanations of the alleged latent dream content."

Not unlike Adler, Stekel writes that "the dream is a sign-post which shows the way to the life conflict. . . . Every dream is a confession, a resurrection of the suppressed, an outcrop of hidden truths."

Always a first-rate scholar, Stekel provides us with a valuable glossary and a detailed index of the hundreds of dreams discussed in the text. This work is the foundation stone of "The Stekel School" of dream analysis, a brilliant effort marked with great insight and erudition.

An English language version, translated by Eden and Cedar Paul, and edited by Emil A. Gutheil, was published in two volumes in 1943 under the title, The Interpretation of Dreams. New Developments and Technique, by Liveright Publishing Company of New York.

Fortschritte is Stekel's last significant contribution to dream and psychoanalytic theory. Stekel fled Vienna only moments before the German occupation of Austria, eventually emigrating to England. But the Nazi successes, the plight of the Jews, and his own ill health proved too much for him. A depressed Wilhelm Stekel, suffering like Freud from terminal cancer, ended his own life on June 27, 1940.

**Stekel (Wilhelm). The Autobiography of Wilhelm Stekel. The Life Story of a Pioneer Psychoanalyst.** Edited by Emil A. Gutheil, M.D. Introduction by Mrs. Hilda Stekel. 293p. index. Liveright. N.Y., 1950.

Interspersed throughout these reminiscences are references to the author's work with specific dreams, demonstrating not only Stekel's theories but also his techniques in therapy which require nowhere near the lengthy sessions demanded in traditional Freudian psychoanalysis. Included are dreams that revealed to Stekel the origins of psychogenic strabismus (squinting), an indication of schizophrenia, and the basis of an intense mother fixation.

**Stevens (Emily H.). Perchance to Dream.** 260p. Pageant-Poseidon Ltd. Brooklyn, N.Y., 1972.

Collection of the author's dreams revealed as experiences to be shared with others. Ms. Stevens pleads guilty to being "an inveterate dreamer," and her dreams, while interesting, are not unusual. There are no attempts at determining meaning, nor any lucid or precognitive dreams revealed. Healthy and wholesome, and therefore quite boring.

**Stevens (William Oliver). The Mystery of Dreams.** 280p. index. Dodd, Mead. N.Y., 1949.

A thorough job of research recording cases of telepathic, clairvoyant, prophetic, and warning dreams. Mr. Stevens researched biographies, autobiographies, the world press and national magazines, recounting dream experiences recorded primarily in the 19th and early 20th centuries.

The author served as a trustee of the American Society for Psychical Research. Because of this, perhaps, he has selected some significant dreams from both American as well as British records, including some personal experiences of his friends. Although he makes no attempt to validate these dreams, the author has excluded some of questionable merit.

The concluding section was most interesting, containing examples of vision dreams, out-of-body-dreams, serial dreams, and dreams of healing. All the standard parapsychological sources are cited, some frequently, including the publications of the Society for Psychical Research, and works by or about J.W. Dunne, Edgar Cayce, and Robert Dale Owen.

While none of this is new, of course, I would want to retain this book for those accounts which had previously escaped my attention. Mr. Stevens' work will not change the mind of a skeptic. Its scientific footing is most unsure. Still it does bring together a number of fascinating examples of parapsychological dreams which might otherwise have gone unrecorded.

**Stevenson (Robert Louis). Across the Plains. With Other Memories and Essays.** 295p. Scribner's. N.Y., 1923.

This fine author has seen fit to include in his collection of miscellaneous writings one fascinating "Chapter on Dreams" in which he writes eloquently on the dream as one of man's most valued treasures. In relating dreams from his own rich storehouse, Stevenson lays before us a vivid panorama of historical vignettes no less impressive than his writings. Indeed, he expends some effort to describe the problems concerning the plotting of his famous novel, Strange Case of Dr. Jekyll and Mr. Hyde, the solution to which came to him in a dream. Here, it seems to me, is a clear example of the dream aiding in the solution of a conscious problem, a validation perhaps of the Adlerian dream theory, at least in one case of artistic creation.

**Stewart (Kilton). Pygmies and Dream Giants.** 295p. map, index. W.W. Norton & Co., N.Y., 1954.

This is the only generally available publication I know

of that was written by the founder (or discoverer) of the Senoi method of dreamwork. Stewart is perhaps the most controversial professional after Freud to contribute to dream research and theory. A brilliant anthropologist and later a psychoanalyst, Stewart began his career by conducting field investigations among the Negrito tribes of Luzon, and Yami tribes of Bataan, both in the Philippines, and among the Senoi (Temiar) tribes of central Malaya.

The results of his efforts were reported in his still unpublished Ph.D. thesis, Magico-Religious Beliefs and Practices in Primitive Societies: A Sociological Analysis of their Therapeutic Aspects, accepted by the University of London in 1948. Stewart's original field research was conducted in Asia over a period of two years in the middle and late 1930s.

In this book, Stewart writes a semi-popular narrative of his experience among the Negritos of Luzon, with scattered sections relating to the role of dreams in Negrito culture. He describes the use of dreams in shamanistic therapy relating to the cure of headaches, the treatment of ringworm, cysts, and other physical maladies, and of the role of the dream in Negrito religion.

In other sections, Stewart discusses the close relationship between trance and dreams, and the appearance of such spirits (earth-spirit, baby-spirit, and father-spirit) in Negrito dreams. In a later paper ("The Dream Comes of Age," Mental Hygiene, vol. 46, 1962), Stewart describes the "parent" dreams of the Negritos. I find no notice of this in his earlier book. According to Stewart, the Negrito "parent" dream indicates that the "dream process is highly amenable to direction, suggestion, example, and other types of education." "The Negrito," he writes, "follows the practice of making sacrifices and prayers to the terrifying dream characters of his children. From year to year the children's dreams become more cluttered with uncontrollable dream characters which push the dreamer around." When illness occurs, he continues, the dreamer is directed "to outface and kill off the offending dream characters who have not been affected by prayers and sacrifices. The dreams of the patient thus directed show a reorganizing and simplifying process as well as the old release process at work."

Dr. Stewart claims that his dreamwork investigations among the Negritos aided him in his subsequent field research among the Senoi of Malaya. Although he considered the Senoi much more advanced in dreamwork than the Negrito, Stewart published no book on his experiences among the Senoi. In addition to his doctoral dissertation, we must rely on a series of scattered articles, principally two on dream theory in Malaysia which appeared in Complex, in the issues of Vol. 6, 1951, and again in Vol. 9, 1953-54.

Two other articles relating to the same topic are titled, "Mental Hygiene and World Peace," and "The Dream Comes of Age," both appearing in Mental Hygiene, Vol. 38, 1954, and Vol. 46, 1962. Stewart contrasts Negrito with Senoi dream practices by noting that where the Negrito essentially releases emotional energy in dreams, the Senoi utilizes dream experiences to make the dream characters work for the dreamer (being a method of unifying their personalitics). The Senoi educate their children through a system of dream education, which "frees the minds of all adult Senoi from the type of rigidity on which crime, mental illness, and psychosomatic diseases are now known to be predicated." The Senoi communicate with the spirits, rocks, trees, rivers, and all things, through dreams. The children are taught the importance of dreams by "educators," whc teach them to face their fears (snakes and tigers) in their dreams, rather than to run away from such fears. From childhood to adult, the Senoi continue to work with their dreams, leading ultimately to a whole and healthy development of both the individual and the tribe as a unit. Senoi dream images and processes enable them to do abstract and symbolic thinking of the highest order. The dream is the principal vehicle in the creation of a rather idyllic tribal setting where there is no crime, no hatred, and no jealousy.

In later years Dr. Stewart began the practice of psychoanalysis in New York and Philadelphia, where he developed Senoi dream workshops in an effort to introduce the western dreamer into the Senoi method of individual fulfillment. Within a few years, particularly in the 1960s and 1970s, the Senoi method was adopted by others as a popular method of group therapy and individual treatment. Articles such as those by Marie C. Doyle, "Enhancing Dream Pleasure with Senoi Strategy," Journal of Clinical Psychology, Vol. 40, March, 1984, began to appear in various professional journals. Senoi dreamwork methods have influenced notable figures in the fields of anthropology, such as Margaret Mead, and in psychoanalysis, as noted in the writings of Harry Stack Sullivan.

Unfortunately, within the last several years some investigators have begun to question the validity of the original data upon which Kilton Stewart built his dream theories. [See in particular the writings of Robert K. Dentan and G. William Domhoff in this bibliography.] Unfortunately, both Pat Noone and Kilton Stewart are dead, so many questions may never be satisfactorily answered.

The effects of the apparent impeachment of the field investigations of Kilton Stewart are certainly destined to discredit the use of Stewart's Senoi methods for many professionals. It is also likely that the better informed writers of popular expositions of dream theory will follow in the footsteps of the scholars. The effectiveness of the Stewart-Senoi technique in dream therapy, however, remains a matter for debate. Reports of positive results must be balanced against the negative effectiveness suggested by such writers as William Domhoff.

**Stewart (Kilton). How to Educate Your Dreams to Work for You.** Stewart Foundation for Creative Psychology. n.p. n.d.

A collection of techniques for using the Senoi method of dreamwork.

**Stewart (Walter A.) & Freeman (Lucy). The Secret of Dreams: A Key to Freudian Dream Analysis.** 224p. Macmillan. N.Y., 1972.

Recommended as a well written, nontechnical introduction to Freudian dream analysis. Utilizes a number of Freud's dreams, accompanied by their interpretation. No footnotes, bibliography or index, but well-formed prose in an easy style. Written by a physician and wife who specialize in interpreting psychoanalysis for the layman.

**Stiles (Percy Goldthwait). Dreams.** 80p. illus. Harvard University Press. Cambridge, 1927.

For those who value the dream diaries of an intelligent, thoughtful, yet "normal" individual, this book is most rewarding. Dr. Stiles writes about his thirty years of recorded dreams. He began his dream diaries in his early twenties, and includes personal dream experiences through his middle fifties.

The writer was a physiologist at the Harvard Medical School, yet he approached his subject from a personal rather than scientific point of view. While Stiles praises the dream theories of Havelock Ellis, and damns those of Sigmund Freud, such is not the main intent of this book. Rather, it is essentially a collection of personal dreams, in which the author demonstrates a kind of childlike acceptance of the natural state of dreaming, seeing in his dreams neither external influences nor internal conflict. He discusses the effect of his bodily condition on dreams, his memories and anticipations, the emotional content of his dreams, and considers the relationship of his own personality to his dreams.

I found the section related to the sensory content of Dr. Stiles' dreams most appealing, particularly his astounding abilities at visual imagery during the dreamstate. All this is made even more exciting by the inclusion of a wondrous collection of black and white, and colored plates, representing some of the finest of the author's remembered dream images.

One regrets that Harvard University Press, now producing prodigious numbers of weighty, scholarly tomes, has all but forgotten the sensitive little books it produced in yesteryear. Percy Stiles' Dreams brightens the soul, and allows our psyches to touch the essence of another human being through the dream.

**Strümpell (L.). Die Natur und Enstehung der Traüme.** 354p. notes. Veit & Co. Leipzig, 1874.

A major late nineteenth century work on dreams which so impressed Sigmund Freud that he quoted from Strümpell no less than eighteen times in his The Interpretation of Dreams. Strümpell's work was widely quoted and was very popular in the pre-Freudian era, presenting one of the most detailed accounts of the complex phenomenon associated with one's inability to remember dreams.

Strümpell examined the weakness and incoherence in most dream images, wondering even how it was possible that the conscious mind remembered the dream at all. He suggests a variety of factors contributing to the forgetting of dreams. The author also delved into the reasons why a dreamer considered his dream to be real, concluding that the soul provides a "dream space" where all distinctions between objective and subjective and a critical sense of causality is suspended. Strümpell's book also includes a section relating to the function of speech in dreams.

**Stuart (Rosa). Dreams and Visions of the War.** 127p. C. Arthur Pearson Ltd. London, 1917.

The British during World War I (unlike World War II, apparently) seem to have produced a number of curious, personal writings on the horrors of the fighting, including many on poetry, and a few on dreams.

One of the more striking of this last genre is this brief dreambook on the war, in which the author supplies numerous fascinating dreams dreamt by soldiers in combat, including those telepathic in nature, and others relating to battlefield apparitions and visions. Some of the most prophetic, however, seem to have been those dreamt by loved ones (mothers and sweethearts) a night or two before receiving official notice that their son or husband had been severely wounded in combat. One also finds that the soldiers remember many instances of battlefield visions and apparitions while awake, few if any explained, but all a product of man's terror and confusion in a hell of sound and fury in which he finds escape impossible.

**Stukane (Eileen). The Dream Worlds of Pregnancy.** 190p. notes, biblio., index. Quill. N.Y., 1985.

A book written for expectant mothers, designed to enable them to gain insights into their dreams, and a better understanding of their emotions and anxieties during pregnancy. The author presents many helpful dreams typical of those in pregnancy, and explains each in careful, simple terms. The book is particularly helpful in showing the differences between dreams during the different stages of pregnancy. Dr. Robert Van de Castle, in his foreword, points to the importance of dreams for women during pregnancy, and makes several interesting observations on the topic, resulting from his earlier research in the field.

**Stumpf (E.F.G.). Der Traum und sein Deutung, nebst erklärten Traumbeispielen.** 188p. notes. Mutze. Leipzig, 1899.

Theoretical discourse arguing that dreams not only have a meaning, but can be interpreted accurately as well. Stumpf believed that such interpretation could best be accomplished through an examination of the symbolism of the dream, particularly its allegorical character. He wrote that his method of interpretation had not yet been proved, however. Freud, in a footnote to his book writes that he had read Stumpf only after his manuscript on The Interpretation of Dreams was completed, but was pleased that Stumpf's theories coincided with his own.

**Sullivan (Harry Stack). Collected Works.** 2 volumes. 2,156p. W.W. Norton. N.Y., 1973.

Considered by many to be one of the most important of American-born psychiatrists, this prolific writer had much to say about the use of dreams in psychiatry as well as dream theory. He differed from Freud, feeling that one could not discover the true content of any dream, particularly since the patient would distort the original in retelling it to the analyst. Since it would be impossible to determine if any dream interpretation were valid, the dream phenomena should be considered personal (not interpersonal) as well as a nonsensory experience, since the dreamer would not actually see, touch, hear, or feel anything during the dream.

Sullivan does not reject the use of dreams in psychotherapy so long as the analyst recognizes these limitations. He would use the dream as an entry into problems of the patient's waking life, the dream then being merely a starting point for discussion.

Of Jungian dream theories, Sullivan has written, that, like many other fashionable theories it is "too preposterous to be taken seriously . . . with its racial unconscious, according to which you are a sort of bud on a great reservoir of God knows quite what, but it is extremely useful for those that it succeeds with." He extends this view to support the dream theories of Kilton Stewart, based upon a forty-five minute discussion with him on the Senoi and their dream psychology (The Fusion of Psychiatry and Social Science by Sullivan, pp. 275-259).

**Sully (James). Illusions: A Psychological Study.** 372p. notes. D. Appleton. N.Y., 1891.

Interesting as a late 19th century view of dreams by a psychologist. Dr. Sully was one of the leading specialists in this area of inquiry, having contributed the section on dreams to the 9th edition of the then still scholarly Encyclopedia Britannica. Sully saw the material making up one's dreams as drawn from waking experiences. These experiences derived primarily from the bodily senses. He devotes considerable attention to the role of internal and external sense stimuli, quoting the results of the investigations of Maury, Strümpell, Meyer, and Wundt.

Sully cites examples of the influence on dream content through experiments of loss of bed covers and cold feet (suggesting the sleeper is walking over snow or ice). Dr. Sully views the preliminary arguments on dream symbolism as "interesting though somewhat fanciful." Although the author suggested that dream life "touches that childish condition of the intelligence which marks the decadence of old age and the encroachments of mental disease," still he argued that most dreams "may properly be classed with the illusions of normal or healthy life, rather than with those of disease."

**Swedenborg (Emanuel). Swedenborg's Journal of Dreams, 1743-1744.** Edited from the original Swedish by G.E. Klemming. Translated into English, 1860, by J.J.G. Wilkinson. Edited by William R. Woofenden. 97p. index. Swedenborg Foundation. N.Y., 1977.

Dream diary of this celebrated Swedish occultist and mystic, including his interpretations interspersed with comments on external life. This diary is important as a record of a continuous dream series (dreams of one person recorded over a period of time) by a creative individual.

A special introduction by Wilson Van Dusen is of value, pointing out that Swedenborg kept this diary for his own personal use, writing his dream record during a critical period while he was in the process of changing from scientist to religious seer. Using dreams to explore his inner processes, Swedenborg experienced visions, trances, and hypnogogic experiences, encountering "The Divine" in many of his dreams. Swedenborg seems also to have used the dream as a form of self-analysis and purification. This is explained in an early dream describing himself as impure and unworthy, and later by the disappearance of all sexual interest at the end of the dream series.

**Symonds (J.A.). Sleep and Dreams.** 93p. Longmans. London, 1851.

Two lectures given by a physician before the Bristol, England Literary and Philosophical Institution. The second lecture is devoted to an analysis of dreams in which the author states that visual images during dreams are frequently accompanied by other sensations such as hearing and smelling. Dreams unrecalled upon waking are sometimes recalled many days later "when their proper associations have chanced to arise."

The author traces most dreams to former and recent experiences, although Dr. Symonds believes that reasoning also takes place during dreams. He dismisses prophetic dreams as but chance occurrences among thousands of dream pictures, though he suggests that dreams have a value as vehicles for remembering facts and events lost to the conscious mind.

**Talayesva (Don C.). Sun Chief. The Autobiography of a Hopi Indian.** Edited by Leo W. Simmons. 460p. illus., index. Yale University Press. New Haven, 1942.

An engrossingly frank autobiography of a Hopi chief struggling with the classic dilemma of ancient ways in conflict with modern society. His fifty-year diary, covering from the 1890s through 1940, is filled with dream references.

The dream played an important role in the life of Chief Talayesva's, for it was in the dream that he made contact with the Hopi gods and goddesses, as well as with the fabled kachina, that mystical being who served as the intermediary between the Hopi and his gods. We find dreams of warning (Chief Talayesva always acted on these), as well as dreams of reincarnation, showing him the fragments of his future life. There were also many bad dreams (nightmares) caused by evil spirits. But, as his grandfather cautioned him in his youth, these could be driven away and their evil effects negated, if one would only spit four times.

A sad and yet delightful writing by a sensitive soul seeking to hold together his tribe's fading way of life.

**Tart (Charles T., editor). Altered States of Consciousness. A Book of Readings.** 575p. biblio., index. Wiley. N.Y., 1969.

A very popular book among college students during the early 1970s. Though possibly more important over the long run, the section on dream consciousness was perhaps less popular than those concerned with psychedelic drugs.

There are five dream papers: "Theories of Dream Formation and Recent Studies of Sleep Consciousness" by David Foulkes, "Toward the Experimental Control of Dreaming: A Review of the Literature" by Charles T. Tart, "A Study of Dreams" by Frederik van Eeden; "The 'High' Dream: A New State of Consciousness" also by Tart, and Kilton Stewart's "Dream Theory in Malaya."

Foulkes' paper concerns a new theory being developed on dream-formation, based upon REM research which Foulkes believes challenges both Freud and Adler on the alleged traumatic instigation of dreams. In this paper we find the beginnings of Foulkes' brilliant theory of cognitive psychological analysis.

The first Tart study reviews REM research as of 1969, while his second gives a preliminary report on high dreams produced by psychedelic chemicals (LSD), with several of the author's dream experiences recorded.

The van Eeden paper was first published in 1913 and records his observations on dreams, including some of his 500 recorded dreams from 1898. He discusses lucid dreams (352 of his were these), as well as flying dreams. A fascinating early study.

Kilton Stewart's paper on Senoi dream psychology may well be the most far reaching, and is now subject to the greatest critical comment. Stewart recounts his visits to the Senoi in the mid-1930s (see Richard Noone's book in this bibliography) and expounds on Senoi dreamwork, which has been the basis of much modern Senoi-oriented dream analysis today.

**Taub-Bynum (E. Bruce). The Family Unconscious. "An Invisible Bond."** 230p. notes, biblio., index. The Theosophical Publishing House. Wheaton, Illinois, 1984.

The psychic field of families is reflected best in dreams, Dr. Taub-Bynum, a psychologist at the Unisity of Massachusetts, believes. In this work on family dynamics and healing, he argues that dreams of individual family members actually establish a pattern which, when observed in their entirety, form an "emotional hologram." The energy within the family dream hologram, the author writes, may someday be tapped in the same way psychotherapists now use dreams in individual therapy.

Taub-Bynum is doing very useful work with a theory that proposes the existence of a "family unconscious."

He also suggests extraordinary forms of communication occur between family members that include bodily movements and speech intonations, and may even include forms of extrasensory perception such as telepathy.

The author's attempt to quantify this data is understandable, though hardly successful. Stanley Krippner, in his foreword to the book, defends this attempt as a requisite to independent observation, while admitting that psychology "has been criticized for slavishly modelling itself after the physical sciences." This is a debate that will forever plague the "science" of psychology, and is one which will certainly not be resolved in this book.

Measurement and methodology aside, Dr. Taub-Bynum has written an important book on a relatively new dimension in the use of dreams. Even the nonspecialist will find his ideas provocative, and the many examples drawn from his own clinical experience, fascinating.

**Tauber (Edward S.) & Green (Maurice R.). Prelogical Experience. An Inquiry Into Dreams & Other Creative Processes.** 196p. index. Basic Books. N.Y., 1959.

Attempt to re-examine the foundations of symbolic theory and those processes in psychoanalytic procedure which deal with the types of experience which have so far not lent themselves to the model of the physical sciences and, so state Tauber and Green, "perhaps never will." The authors explore the prelogical processes and those forms of communication that operate below the levels of awareness. These include ESP, perceptual experience, subthreshold phenomena, and dreams and dream analysis. The book ends with a chapter, "The Dream as a Message." This is a fascinating work, in which the authors seek to expand the present limits of theoretical knowledge, projecting new concepts and values. Those sections relating to dreams, while aimed primarily at the psychoanalyst, still deserve wide readership, particularly among those who question whether the dream is really important as a guide to the inner psyche.

**Taylor (Eugene). William James on Exceptional Mental States. The 1896 Lowell Lectures.** 222p. notes, index. Scribner's. N.Y., 1983.

Critical re-creation of James' previously unpublished Lowell Lectures, the first being titled "Dreams and Hypnotism," which focused on the "hypnagogic state," i.e., the twilight region between waking and sleeping. More for James' fans than dreamworkers.

**Taylor (Jeremy). Dream Work. Techniques for Discovering the Creative Power in Dreams.** Introduction by Ann Faraday. 280p. bibliography. Paulist Press. N.Y., 1983.

The author, a Unitarian Universalist minister practicing in the San Francisco area, has long had an interest in dreams, and has worked with individuals and groups using his own dreamwork techniques. This book is based on two earlier monographs, Basic Hints for Dream Work (1980) and Nurturing the Creative Impulse (1982). In Dream Work Taylor describes his ideas and methods for using dreams as a vehicle both for exploring the unconscious, as well as for solving individual and social problems.

Taylor writes in an easy, interesting style, and the sum total of his effort is an excellent popular exposition of the dream and its potential. He explains the practice and techniques of dream recall, points out ways to understand one's dreams, and even provides a how-to-do-it manual on group dream work. Taylor's interests range from encountering archetypes in dreams to lucid dreaming to the potential of dream yoga. Ann Faraday, in her excellent introduction, points out that the author presents "dream work as the missing link between the age-old religious ideal of love and its practical realization."

There is much here to profit and intrigue the beginner interested in understanding and benefiting from dreams. Like many popularizers of dreamwork, Taylor may be a bit too enthusiastic with regard to the potential benefits that might accrue from such techniques as lucid dreaming. This is only a minor fault in a work brimming with good information and bright prospects. Dream Work ends with a valuable, annotated bibliography.

**Tedlock (Barbara). Time and the Highland Maya.** 245p. notes, biblio. index. University of New Mexico Press. Albuquerque, 1982.

Religious practices of the present-day Quiché Indians in the highlands of Guatemala examined by a noted ethnologist whose fieldwork involved being initiated into the practice of Quiché shamanism. The dream plays a major role in the religion and life of the Quiché. Dr. Tedlock reveals that some shamans receive messages during dreams via sensations in their hands and legs, or in the form of voices and sounds. The dream, in fact, is one of the classical methods (the others being sickness, ecstasy, and inheritance) of being named a Mayan diviner, or shaman.

Many Mayan shaman priests are not only selected by the nature of their dreams, but prescribe herbs and other techniques for ridding their patients of illness on the basis of the dream. Most dream interpretation on the other hand, is taught indirectly "through mythtelling, prayer-making, and dream analysis, but above all through direct discussion of the movements actually experienced by the novice and the teacher while they are together." The emphasis in Time and the Highland Maya is on the relationship of time to the Maya, as well as the role of the dream and other factors governing the selection and training of Quiché shamans.

**Tedlock (Barbara, editor). Dreaming: The Anthropology and Psychology of the Imaginal.** Cambridge University Press. Cambridge, England. [Projected publication date: 1987].

Barbara Tedlock is one of the foremost original thinkers in cross-cultural dream research today. Her chapter that leads off this collection, "Dreaming and Dream Research," may be the best single exposition of the meaning and role of the dream published in recent years.

Dr. Tedlock's writing is a critical summarization of man's knowledge of the meaning of the dream at this juncture in our history. She fills a scant forty-five pages with a wealth of data and interpretation, ranging from a clear explanation of the idea of the dream through the centuries and among differing cultures, to a precise synthesization of the key issues separating traditional psychotherapists from laboratory experimentalists. Her paper concludes with a set of largely unconsidered factors that require us to reconsider many of our current theories of the dream and its interpretation.

The author mines recent ethnographical field research on the role of the dream in primitive cultures, then relates this to what she terms "the dream problem" in modern American society. She argues persuasively that the social context in which the dream is reported to others may be as important as the dream itself.

After showing how the dream is used in primitive cultures, Dr. Tedlock writes that we suffer in our modern scientific culture from social and cultural blinders that dictate what we think and do with our dreams.

Dr. Tedlock's incisive analysis touches the debate between the philosophers and the psychologists over the received view of dreaming, and the Malcolm/ Wittgenstein argument that dreams cannot be considered experiences in the same sense that conscious mental phenomena are experienced. Her synthesis and interpretation of modern REM research demonstrates to this reviewer that our laboratory scientists will never discover the ultimate truths about the dream so long as they work in isolation from the dream's cultural, social, and personal significance.

The author argues that the presently favored cognitive theory of dreams suffers from "the American stereotype of the meaninglessness of dreams," but looks with more approval on the recently reported discoveries by Canadian researchers that the major function of dreaming is to be noticed. This discovery, if valid, fits in logically with evidence being gathered by modern ethnologists.

Dr. Tedlock identifies chinks in the armor not only of the experimentalists, but of the earlier schools of anthropologists, questioning the methodology of many of the field researchers themselves. The author also takes to task both anthropologists and psychologists who devoted their work to the enumeration, analysis, and tabulation of the manifest content of dreams. Her critique covers not only the work of Eggan, Griffith, and Sears among the anthropological community, but Hall, Nordby and Van de Castle in the psychological fraternity as well.

All these efforts suffer from methodological and interpretative weaknesses according to Tedlock, in the failure of the investigators to expand their own narrow disciplinary horizons. Psychologists ignore, she writes, the fact that their study of the dreaming experience is partially dependent on their subjects' communication of such experiences by culturally determined means. Anthropologists, on the other hand, "ignore the fact that dream communication in other cultures is partially dependent on native theories about the dream experience."

Dr. Tedlock cautions anthropologists that investigations into the dream in any culture must contain not only the actual dream report, but also the nature of the dream theory in that particular society, embracing "theories and ways of sharing including the relevant discourse frames," as well as the cultural mode of dream interpretation in that society.

The heart of Dr. Tedlock's paper, it seems to me, is to underline the largely ignored fact that dream interpretation is a "communicative" process, and that thinking about dreaming is a "psychodynamic communicative process," in which no single dream or group of dreams can be interpreted solely in accordance with any set theory now in practice. This new psychodynamic approach to dreaming has far-reaching implications.

Barbara Tedlock is a professor of anthropology at Tufts University and a fellow at the prestigious Institute for Advanced Study at Princeton. The eleven papers in this collection are a product of a seminar held in late 1982 at the School of American Research in Santa Fe, New Mexico. This seminar was proposed and structured by Dr. Tedlock. Her idea was to discard old methodologies in favor of a critique of past approaches and an offering of new alternatives. If Dr. Tedlock's paper is representative, she has achieved her purpose.

I have not had access to the ten remaining papers in this collection, and the following summary is derived from Dr. Tedlock's introductory paper. In his work on the dreams of the Aguaruna of Peru, Michael Brown finds that while dreams play a prominent role in daily decision-making, they are viewed more as possibilities than as accomplished realities. Bruce Mannheim, in his linguistic analysis, finds that the Andean peoples of southern Peru treat dreams figuratively at the narrative level but literally in their lexicon of dream signs. In a field study with the Kagwahiv of Brazil, Waud Kracke discovered they use a single linguistic form in the narration of dreams, regardless of whether the images are to be interpreted metaphorically or literally.

Gilbert Herdt, in his field work with the Sambia of New Guinea, concentrated on the experience of dream sharing, in which the phenomenology of the dream world of the Sambia parallels the secular world. The Sambia draw a distinction between the soul (or unconscious) that directly experiences the dream, and the "thought" that relays the images of the dream world and interprets them metaphorically.

The Kalapalo of Brazil, on the other hand, seem to separate the dreamer's "self" from the direct experience of the dream. The Kalapalo, according to the paper by Ellen Basso, experience dreams through a hidden personal reality only incoherently perceived in waking life. William Merrill, in his study of the Rarámuri Indians of Mexico, writes that dream facts and events are described as real events taking place in the external world, although these same peoples would not act on the message in a dream without other, real world, supportive data.

The collection also contains a paper by John Homiak on Rastafarian visionary dreams, Benjamin Kilborne's analysis of the importance of relating dream reports and interpretations to specific social settings, and a paper on the frequently overlooked interface between waking and dreaming consciousness by Douglass Price-Williams. The editor, Barbara Tedlock, has also contributed one other paper to this collection, treating the process of dream sharing and interpretation among the Zuñi and Quiché Indians.

A bright theorist in dream theory and practice once wrote that the answer to the meaning of dreams may come ultimately from the study of anthropology. If so, Barbara Tedlock may be the one to find that answer.

**Teillard (Ania). Ce que disent les rêves.** 225p. notes, indices. Stock. Paris, 1970.

An interesting Jungian examination of dream symbolism originally published under the title Le Symbolisme du rêve in 1944. Dr. Teillard discusses symbolism of space, colors, names, and music, then examines the feminine symbols as revealed in dreams of mother, land, and moon, and the masculine symbols of father, sun, sky, lion, serpent, and dragon. A final chapter is concerned with the concept of transformation. The book contains several hundred dreams accompanied by an analysis of their symbols.

**Te Paske (Bradley A.). Rape and Ritual. A Psychological Study.** 157p. notes, illustrations, bibliography, index. Inner City Books. Toronto, 1982.

Dr. Te Paske, a practicing Jungian analyst, begins with a historical and legal review of the history of rape, then examines the modern feminist attitude towards it. He provides a complex analysis of the psychological dimension of rape, interweaving theory, case material, mythology, and dreams. Some will find this book disturbing and the ideas are not always easy to follow, but Te Paske's insights, particularly his analysis of the archetypes at work, are based on firm Jungian footing.

**Thibodeau (Robert). The Hermetic Dream.** Hermes Press. Detroit, 1978.

Seeks to relate the dream to astrology and the occult. The earlier writings on dream interpretation by Madame Blavatsky and Francis Mayer are included here.

**Thorndike (Lynn). A History of Magic and Experimental Science.** 8 volumes. notes, bibliographic references, indices. Macmillan & Co. and Columbia University Press. N.Y., 1923-1958.

A truly monumental study tracing human knowledge during the first 1600 years of the modern era. During these centuries scientific thought consisted largely of philosophical and mystical studies, fusing legend, magic, alchemy, divination, astrology, imagination, superstition, and pure speculation.

This great eight volume work of erudition occupied over fifty years of Dr. Thorndike's working life, and its product is an amazing amount of scholarship which is apparent on every page. Each volume contains data on dreams. Much is of evidentiary as well as of historical interest, since each bit and piece of data fits like a fragment into a giant jigsaw puzzle leading to what we know today as the science of dreams.

Volumes I and II cover the first thirteen centuries of the Christian era. Our dream knowledge begins largely with the physician Galen, whose collected works number a prodigious 21 volumes, very little of which has been translated into English. Among those is his Diagnosis From Dreams, possibly the earliest serious analysis of dream interpretation as a guide to the symptoms of specific illnesses. At the other extreme we encounter Nectabenus, whose legend was widespread through the Middle Ages. Nectabenus, was dream interpreter and diviner to Olympias, wife of King Philip of Macedonia. As practitioner of the arcane art of "dream incubation transference," Nectabenus designed dreams for Olympias, bathing a wax image of the Queen in a herbal potion, then reciting a litany of special dream incantations.

One of the most learned men of the twelfth century, John of Salisbury, wrote Polycraticus, in which he discussed the seasons of the year when one dreams best, and discussed the ideal place for dreaming, as well as the type of personality best suited to dreaming. John, however, rejected dream divination, calling it the work of the devil. In fact he saw many dreams as the work of demons. The then very popular manuscript, Dream-Book of Daniel did not escape John's condemnation, and he cautioned the reader to cast it aside. John believed that dream interpretation was no art at all, or an idle one at best. He warned too against blasphemy in dreamwork, cautioning "Whoever fastens his credulity to the significations of dreams evidently wanders as far from sincere faith as from the path of reason."

Volumes III and IV treat the 14th and 15th centuries. In these Dark Ages a few friars were burned at the stake for producing manuscripts on medical astrology, while others perished for speculating on dreamwork not sanctioned by the Holy Church. Petrarch, one of the more noteworthy scholars of the era, agreed with Cicero in rejecting any and all dream interpretation. Petrarch rejected even his own dream experiences. At one time he dreamed of the death of a distant friend, only to find out later that his friend had died at the moment of the dream. Taking warning from another dream, he saved a comatose friend from being buried alive. Even so, Petrarch insisted that all dream prognostications, including his own, were but "mere coincidences." All in all, serious dream investigation seems to have stagnated during the Dark Ages. Most of the writings that still exist suggest that the Devil or devils cause dreams. The one or two odd manuscripts devoted entirely to dreams essentially repeat the dream theories of Aristotle.

A general resurgence of dreamwork appears in Volumes V and VI, which are devoted to the 16th Century. Jerome Cardan, a leading philosopher of the century, wrote a refutation of traditional Aristotelian views that some dreams are true while others are false. All are true, Cardan held, since all are nothing more than "marvelous properties of nature." Cardan attempted a prescientific approach to dreamwork, breaking dreams down into different categories, and including scientific rather than popular dream symbols in his writings. He even included select samples of his own dreams, taken apparently from his daily dream diaries.

The 16th Century is the first century of the printed book, and there soon began a flow of books on dream interpretation. The traditional favorites of earlier centuries, The Dream Book of Daniel and The Dreams of Solomon appear in published form for the first time, as did the writings of Artemidorus, which was first printed from the manuscript in 1518. In addition, Synesius of Cyrene's book on dreams appears.

While most of the foregoing are essentially the first printing of earlier manuscript editions of dream dictionaries, some effort was made to begin at least a prescientific approach to dreamwork. One book was authored by the religious philosopher, Ferdinand Ponzetti, first president of the Papal Apostolic Camera. Ponzetti's dream speculations were more religious and philosophical than substantive. Dreams, he wrote, come from the "intelligences," and from "strange influences," while others appear from "idols cast off from objects." Ponzetti found dream interpretation both "complicated and difficult." Such was only natural, however, "because the senses even while awake are deceived by hallucinations and much more so in sleep." Ponzetti argued that since images are not formed in the same way by different people, so dream images and their interpretation must differ between one person and another. Dream interpreters, he wrote, must keep in mind that individual dream interpretations will vary, just as would external influences such as climate and the position of the stars. While concluding that dream interpretation would never reach the level of exactness as grammar or medicine, Ponzetti nevertheless wrote that it would be an error to ignore the value of dream interpretation. His writings include a five page dictionary of dream symbols.

The final two volumes of Dr. Thorndike's massive compendium, Volumes VII and VIII, present the sum of human knowledge and science as of the 17th Century. Here, for the first time, we find both philosophers and scientists seeking to come to grips with dreams in the more modern sense. Descartes, the leading philosopher of that period, attributed his ideas to either subsconscious cerebration during the dream state, or to conscious thought as he lay in bed after waking in the morning. University scholars of the 17th century began an approach to dream interpretation which antedated Freud and Jung.

A leader in this pioneering research was Bartholomaeus

Keckermann (1571-1609), a professor at Heidelberg and Danzig, who turned out a prodigious number of texts and "systems" in his short lifetime. One was devoted to dreams. In his third book in The Physical System, Keckermann wrote that dreams were of a divine or diabolic origin, and could arise from "the influx of the stars, when the brain is affected by moonbeams shining into the bedroom or by some arcane influence of other celestial bodies, especially by the juxtaposition of the planet Mercury with the moon." His views were not inconsistent with two Italian professors, Bartholomaeus Mastrius of Meldola and Bonaventura Bellutus of Catania, who both noted the influence of the stars on dreams as on good grapes and the making of fine wine. These Italian scholars suggested that dreams would be particularly useful as guides not only to the weather, but to good health.

Richard Sanders, an English writer, attempted to develop a system of dream interpretation based upon a fusion of choromancy and geomancy in his book published in 1653. Even so, Sanders concluded that dreams seldom served as accurate predictors of future events. Perhaps the most interesting effort was undertaken by Jacobus Masenius in his Mirror of Images of Occult Truth, published in 1650. Masenius suggested that dreams offered different images to different people, depending upon their physical and mental dispositions. He too argued that dream interpretations differ according to the dreamer. Significantly Masenius wrote that a physician could discern universal symbols from dreams indicative of a disease or physical impairment. These same symbols, he speculated, might also signify "unified occult truths."

I regret that this review has not begun to do full justice to the significant scholarly effort of Dr. Thorndike, which makes a major contribution by tracing the development of early dream theories. One finds a rich body of translations of materials not generally available, complemented by a nearly exhaustive collection of informative annotations and bibliographic entries. While the indices to the first two volumes are excellent, those in later volumes are less so, suggesting to me that someone other than the author is responsible for this failing. Still, these limitations are minor.

Every student of early dreamwork will find in these pages a splendid opportunity to spend many a wondrous night deep in the research of arcane dream lore and speculation during sixteen centuries of thought and writing on dreams.

**Thurston (Mark A.). How to Interpret Your Dreams. Practical Techniques Based on the Edgar Cayce Readings.** 192p. A.R.E. Press, Virginia Beach, Virginia, 1978.

Explanation of Edgar Cayce's theories of and techniques for dream interpretation, with suggestions for self-interpretation in order to achieve emotional and spiritual betterment. Dr. Thurston quotes extensively from original Cayce readings, and provides the reader with practical exercises in doing his or her own dreamwork.

Thurston's book is well written and easily read. His claims are neither outrageous nor should they frighten off readers not familiar with Cayce's methods. Dr. Thurston's book is recommended by the Association for Research and Enlightenment in its dream courses, and has gone through at least six printings.

**Tichner (Edward Bradford). Primer of Psychology.** 314p. index. Macmillan. N.Y., 1898.

This text by an American psychologist at Cornell University represents the accepted physiological and sense-oriented theory of dreams common in the late 19th century. It was published two years before Freud's important work, and is significant less for what it says than as an indication of the standard of accepted scientific thinking on the dream in the years immediately before Freud.

Tichner, relying extensively on the writings of William James, Sully, and Wundt, considered the dream to be an abnormal state of consciousness, "a deviation from the rule or norm of function in a sound cortex." Dreams are the product of sensory stimulation. He writes that illogical and fantastic dream images appear because of "the total lapse of attention," which is a primary difference between sleep and waking. Dreams, however, are not entirely disorderly, since they abide by the law of association.

Dr. Tichner mentions neither the unconscious nor symbolism in dreams. He writes that since all dreams are a product of the physiological rather than psychological process, any attempted interpretation would be meaningless and of no scientific interest.

**Tipu Sultan. The Dreams of Tipu Sultan.** Translated from the Original Persian with an introduction and notes by Mahmud Husain. 106p. illus. [Pakistan Historical Society Pbln. 7] Karachi, n.d.

Early dream diary by a Moslem leader in India killed by the British in 1799. After his death, the British unearthed a hidden manuscript in Tipu Sultan's palace which contained thirty-seven dreams recorded between 1785 and 1798.

This dream diary reflects the dream content of a brilliant political and military leader, and a devout

Moslem, whose single purpose in life was the protection of his kingdom from his enemies.

A majority of the dreams dealt with Tipu Sultan's wars against the British and their allies, many giving tidings of successes and victory. Others dwelt upon his life and veneration for Moslem saints. A small number of Tipu Sultan's dreams were followed by his own interpretations. In one, Tipu Sultan interpreted a woman in a man's dress as his enemy, against whom he was warring at the time. In another dream, he saw three silver trays of fresh dates as representing three enemies, the British and two of their allies, whom he hoped would fall into his hands.

**Tissie (P.). Les Rêves, physiologie et pathologie.** 190p. Ed. Clairie. Paris, 1870.

Tissie presents an interesting early thesis on the role of dreams in medicine. He considered dreams to be obscure, if at times accurate, guides to both physical and mental illnesses, and also found a direct relationship between dreams and psychosis. Dr. Tissie also argued that certain bodily organs were responsible for specific dream content, and that it was possible for the physician to undertake a preliminary diagnosis of a particular physical ailment based on the patient's dream. The early work of this Paris physician influenced Freud in the development of his dream theories.

**Tobowolska (Justine). Etude sur les illusions de temps dans les rêves du sommeil normal.** Thesis. Paris, 1900.

This dissertation is concerned with the passage of time during dreams. It was cited by Freud.

**Torda (C.). Memory and Dreams. A Modern Physics Approach.** 451p. illus. notes, biblio. Walters Publishers. Chicago, 1980.

Professor Torda, a physicist and physician, employs what he terms the ponto-geniculo-occipital wave complex to measure the value of REM research. Torda is also preoccupied with proving or disproving Freud's theories through this process. Among his conclusions is the contention that dreaming is not pertinent for memory consolidation, but uses retrieved memory traces and may represent a second exposure that facilitates remembering. The author states that the dependence of dreaming upon circadian processes invalidates Freud's concept that dreams originate with id problems, while he also concludes that he has validated Freud's theory that the dream is the protector of sleep.

Dr. Torda has certainly researched what appears to be an amazing number of sources. The bibliography alone runs to over seventy-two pages. The pages are riddled with a profusion of charts, graphs, formulas, and schematics. This may be a book of great erudition, providing the reader with a fresh, scientific approach to the meaning of dreams. I am not qualified to judge.

**Tress (Arthur). Arthur Tress. The Dream Collector.** Text by John Minahan. photos. Avon. N.Y., 1972.

Tress talked to children about their dreams, then attempted to duplicate their imagery through photography. The result is largely a macabre series of gruesome scenes more reminiscent of nightmares. There is scant narrative about the dreams or dreamers, and one hopes that these are not the standard dreams of New York children.

**Tridon (Andre). Psychoanalysis, Sleep and Dreams.** 161p. biblio. Knopf. N.Y., 1921.

Psychoanalyst's attempt to correlate sleep and dreams by explaining sleep through dreams. The author's thesis is that "we sleep in order to dream and to be for a number of hours our simpler and unrepressed selves." Dr. Tridon regards sleeplessness as a product of our fear of incompletely repressed cravings, fearing the primitive self which comes through the unconsciousness of sleep. Nightmares are repressed cravings which seek gratification under a symbolic cloak and, although they torture us with fear, we fail to recognize their true meaning.

The author discusses wish fulfillment in dreams, daydreams, recurrent dreams, neurosis and dreams, and dream interpretation. The author's interpretation of prophetic dreams is Freudian, suggesting their unreliability because of our "treacherous and unreliable" memory of our dreams, and suggests that all are cases of wish fulfillment. Recurrent dreams, on the other hand, reflect the leading motif of the dreamer's waking life. Such dreams, Dr. Tridon believes, may give valuable indications of physical trouble as, for example, tooth dreams which suggest the need to have the dreamer's teeth examined for decay. Dreams of animals gnawing at some organ, similarly, may be indicative of cancerous development, while dreams of exhaustion from climbing hills often suggest heart disease.

In his rules of dream interpretation Dr. Tridon warns against interpreting one's own dreams or attempting to interpret a single dream (20 or 30 are needed). He draws on numerous dream examples from Freud as well as from his own practice. Somewhat dated, but still of interest and value, particularly for the many dream interpretations given of actual cases.

**Tryon (Thomas). Pythagoras. His Mystick Philosophy Revived or the Mystery of Dreams Unfolded.** 299p. Tho. Salisbury. London, 1691.

This late 17th century work represents an important early attempt to consider dreams scientifically. Hence the mention of Pythagoras in the title, serving we are told, as a model for the author's methodology. Tryon believed there was a universal reason for dreams. That purpose was so that man's spirit, "being in the image of the creator who never sleeps," could encounter him in the dream state, viewing him as an "adorable, divine architype [first use of this term in relationship to dreams?] . . . eminating and reflecting ideas of love and complacency."

The author allowed for six basic types of dreams: those based on the "constitution or complexion of each particular person"; those deriving from everyday life or "these things which he is most earnestly intent upon, or concerned about in the daytime"; those caused by possible changes in planetary cycles; confused dreams arising from diet, medicine, or "an abundance of vapours to the brain"; dreams initiated by the Angel of Darkness or evil spirits; dreams representing visitations from Angels; and those dreams containing revelations from God.

Tryon suggested that different personalities might experience different dreams. Individuals of sanguine, choleric, or melancholy personalities would have dreams reflecting their personalities. Those exhibiting multiple or many personality characteristics, would experience combination or varying dreams.

Only through the dream state, the author argued, could man communicate with the spirits. "Now dreams are no other than certain discourses and incorporeal sights of the soul," he wrote, "being in sleep, loosed from the heavy fetters of the body, whereby it hath an near affinity with the material beings, and according to what property of the sevenfold nature he is subject unto, such and such fantasies, representations, or dreams . . . which appear as real as if they were corporeal qualities, and the soul is thereby either tormented, and full of perplexity, or on the other side filled with joy and delight" (pp. 194-5).

In an appendix on madness, Thomas Tryon suggests that "there being an affinity or analogy between dreams and madness . . . the understanding of one will illustrate the other." There is much here that antedates the views of Freud, Jung, and even Adler. Regretfully, none of these gentlemen appear to have consulted the writings of Thomas Tryon.

**Tryon (Thomas). A Treatise of Dreams and Visions.** 306p. T. Sowle. London, 1695.

More of a religious and personal orientation than the preceding title. The first edition of this work appeared in 1689. Tryon discusses the self-generated dream, when the body is in its natural passivity of sleep, "the soul is free to dream, that is, to shake off the fetters of the senses, to be on the wing in the suburbs of Eternity." Through the dream, the author writes, one can visit remote countries and celestial spheres. Dreams and visions, he postulated, are God's "wonderful communications with his servants." Through God's intervention in the dreamworld, man's soul might be healed through the dream.

**Turner (Julia). The Psychology of Self-Consciousness.** 243p. glossary. Kegan, Paul, Trench. London, 1923.

The author criticizes Freud's dream theories because of his supposed failure to distinguish properly between consciousness and self-consciousness. Turner argues that human beings, unlike animals, are self-conscious, which means conflict and anxieties exist in a state which is essentially the opposite of sense perception. A complex theory, complexly presented.

**Twitchell (Paul) & Gross (Darwin). The Eck-Ynari. The Secret Knowledge of Dreams.** 212p. index. Eckankar. Menlo Park, Calif., 1980.

A dream interpretation handbook used by followers of Eckankar, a mystical religious movement that claims to trace its origins to Tibetan texts written by a tribe that populated a region in what is today Western China. The movement, founded by Paul Twitchell, utilizes the dream state as a method of "soul travel," in a system not far removed from that practiced by Yogis and Buddhists.

In spite of this esoteric setting, the Eckankar advocates have had success in attracting a rather significant following, particularly among the intellectuals in university communities. Many report success using Eckankar dream techniques, especially as a tool for achieving self-realization and happiness.

**Tylor (Edward B.). Primitive Culture. Researches Into the Development of Mythology, Philosophy, Religion, Language, Art, and Custom.** 2 volumes. 502;471p. notes. bibliography, index. Brentano's. London, 1871.

Contains perhaps the earliest attempt at cross-cultural analysis of primitive peoples. Tylor observes that even in healthy waking life the primitive never learned to make a rigid distinction between the subjective and objective, between imagination and reality. This is particularly evident in dreams, where little if any distinction is made between dream imagery and waking reality. Tylor discusses the significance of dreams in a wide variety of primitive cultures, including the Zulus, Karens, early Greenlanders, Australian aborigines, and the Kamchadals of Russia.

He notes that the interpretation of dream symbols in any culture may be most difficult, since many turn on cultural keys which would have to be known in order to understand the dream symbol. He cites the Moslem interpretation of eggs in a dream to be concerned with women, largely because Mohammed wrote that a women was like an egg hidden in a nest. He also points out that the meaning of symbols change as the culture changes, and were sometimes invented to reflect the obvious meaning of the dream.

In many primitive societies, Tylor observed that the dream was utilized as an exit for the soul. The Karens of Burma believed that the wandering soul sees and experiences private journeys after it has left the body. On the other hand, the Karens believed that the soul can only visit places the body has visited in an earlier period. In other cases, the soul may enter and visit the sleeper during the dream state, particularly the soul of a departed friend or relative. This is a common belief among the Fiji, Zulu, and certain North American Indian tribes.

Tylor writes of an interesting form of reverse wish fulfillment interpretation, and is one of the first to use the term. The Zulus, for example, had learned in their hard life of the fallacy of expecting fulfillment of promises experienced in dreams. So they reversed their interpretations to correspond to reality. Thus, if one dreams of death, the grave, or funeral rites, then it means that he will not die since he has already dreamed his death. Similarly, to dream of a wedding dance is to dream of death. The Maoris of New Zealand followed a similar form of reverse interpretation, suggesting that to dream of the recovery of a dying relative means the actual death of that relative.

One of Tylor's more significant observations is that myths derive from animism which, in turn, is a product of dreams. In this respect, the author was perhaps the first to tie the myth closely to the dream.

Edward Tylor's book has been reprinted many times, and he is frequently quoted in scholarly works, even today. While the author touched but lightly on the role of dreams in primitive cultures, his pioneering effort is remembered. Primitive Culture stands as an important historical beginning to modern cross-cultural investigation.

**Uhr (Leonard) & Miller (James G., editors). Drugs and Behavior.** 676p. notes, biblio., index. Wiley. N.Y., 1960.

One paper in this collection concerns dreams: "Drugs and Dreams" by Roy M. Whitman, Chester M. Pierce and James Maas. In a clinical setting, the authors reviewed twenty-six dreams of one patient over eight nights before and after being administered meprobamate (Miltown). They found that "... the dreams before medication could not be distinguished from those during medication."

**Ullman (Montague) & Krippner (Stanley). Dream Studies and Telepathy. An Experimental Approach.** 119p. illus., notes. [Parapsychological Monographs, No. 12] Parapsychology Foundation. N.Y., 1970.

Preliminary report by two recognized experimenters in parapsychology relating their experiments conducted on dreams and telepathy at the Maimonides Medical Center dream research laboratory in Brooklyn, New

York. Much of the research was funded by the National Institute of Mental Health, marking the first U.S. government support of a project designed to investigate the potential of dream telepathy.

The report begins with a brief review of the potential of telepathy during dreams, and discusses other recent research on dreams conducted in controlled laboratory environments. The Ullman/Krippner experiments are detailed, with the authors concluding that a correlation existed between dreams and telepathy at "statistically significant levels."

**Ullman (Montague) & Krippner (Stanley). Dream Telepathy.** With Alan Vaughan. 300p. notes, illus., index. Macmillan. N.Y., 1973.

In this expanded and revised version of the previous title, Ullman and Krippner hold firm to their opinion that dream telepathy is more than just a theory, even though they admit that their own laboratory experiments ended with mixed results. They conclude that "the experimental evidence for dream telepathy buttresses clinical evidence . . . that [dream telepathy] is far more subtle and complicated than current psychoanalytic and behavioral theory suggest."

Ullman and Krippner began their experiments with the working hypothesis that ESP occurs more frequently in dreams than in the conscious state. Much of their experimental effort sought to find out whether a telepathic stimulus might build up over one or more nights, and whether they could demonstrate any sign of dream telepathy between agent and the dreamer.

It is significant that the experimenters found certain subjects more "telepathic" than others. One of the most sensitive of these was Robert Van de Castle, now one of the leading dream research professionals in the United States. One wonders if the subject is not equally important to an experiment of this nature as is the design of the experiment itself. Perhaps this explains why the Maimonides investigators were criticized in a scholarly journal pointing out that later, independent experiments, following the same model and controls, had failed to duplicate the findings of Ullman and Krippner. No less depressing, is the continuing prejudice within the scientific community against any form of research into the parapsychological aspects of the dream.

For whatever the reason, there has been a dramatic flagging of interest in ESP and dream telepathy over the past decade, especially in the laboratory. Funds for such research, either governmental or private, are all but nonexistent. Today Montague Ullman practices his vocation by leading experiential dream workshops, while Stanley Krippner survives by putting his peripatetic skills to use in a variety of engaging activities. Both, unfortunately, are no longer connected with experimental parapsychological research.

I would suspect that the only real effort in dream telepathy research today is being conducted in the Soviet Union. Should the normally secretive Russians reveal positive findings in this area, I would anticipate a revival in American parapsychological research. Meanwhile, the book Dream Telepathy stands as the best objective source we have today. Partisans and detractors alike will find it absorbing and rewarding.

**Ullman (Montague) & Zimmerman (Nan). Working With Dreams.** 355p. notes, index. Delacorte Press. N.Y., 1979.

Possibly the best general book now available explaining the nuts and bolts of dreamwork for the individual and group. Dr. Ullman has been one of the leading authorities on the dream for the last several decades and Ms. Zimmerman is a professional writer and avid lay dreamworker. The language is simple, the organization logical, and the content clear and exciting. Recommended for all interested in a nontechnical introduction to the subject.

**Ullrich (M.W.). Der Schlaf und das Traumleben, Geisteskraft.** Berlin, 1896.

**Unger (F.). Die Magie des Traumes als Unsterblich-Keitsbeweis.** Munster, 1898.

**Uttley (Alison). The Stuff of Dreams.** 255p. Faber & Faber. London, 1953.

I am amazed that Alison Uttley, a widely published British author of children's books, has begun and ended with but one book on dreams. We find here the best taken from her dream journals over a period of roughly twenty years.

These include eight prognostic dreams, five beautiful "fairy-tale" dreams, six flying and journey dreams, eight dreams of the supernatural, eight nightmares, eight "scientific" dreams, and a host of others.

I can readily understand how Alison Uttley came to write almost half a hundred wondrous little tales for little people; I cannot forgive her, however, for inviting us into her wondrous world of dreams, then cutting us off without further word or explanation.

**Valentine (Charles Wilfred). Dreams and the Unconscious. An Introduction to the Study of Psycho-Analysis.** 144p. biblio. Macmillan. N.Y., 1922.

Popular explanation of Freud's theory of the unconscious with particular reference to its role in dream interpretation. Dr. Valentine explains psychoanalysis through dreams and devotes two chapters to the psychology of dreams. Of Freudian orientation, but with mention of the expansion of Freudian concepts by Carl Jung and others. Based upon the author's lectures given between 1919 and 1920 before the Socratic Society of Birmingham University.

**Van de Castle (Robert L.). The Psychology of Dreaming.** Large format. 46p., in double columns. bibliography. General Learning Press. Morristown, N.J., 1971.

Perhaps the best single, introductory exposition on dreaming. This book was widely used as a textbook for college psychology courses, but is unfortunately dated. Still The Psychology of Dreaming is highly recommended to those interested in the application of dream theory and techniques to modern psychology. It presents in a very few words the ideas, concepts, and developments in the field of dreams that many more weighty tomes fail to do in many more pages. The writing is clear and interesting, and the synthesis, impressive.

Dr. Robert Van de Castle is another of the important pioneers in dream research whose reputation is largely unknown beyond his peers. Yet his contributions to the field of dream theory and practice are substantial. Dr. Van de Castle was an early participant in the experiments on the parapsychological potential of dreaming conducted at the Maimonides Laboratory, and joined Calvin Hall in the formulation of the first serious attempt to quantify the content of dreams.

Robert Van de Castle is currently a clinical psychologist and professor at the University of Virginia

School of Medicine. He is president of the Association for the Study of Dreams, the only professional society in this field, and is also co-editor and publisher of the Dream Network Bulletin. In addition to lecturing and offering joint seminars with Dr. Henry Reed on dream incubation techniques, he is also involved in a near-exhaustive project, establishing a computer base for all significant ideas and sources on the dream. It is small wonder that he has found no time to revise The Psychology of Dreaming.

**Vande Kemp (Hendrika). The Dream in Periodical Literature, 1860-1910.** 515p. notes, biblio. University Microfilm Editions. Ann Arbor, Michigan, 1977.

This doctoral dissertation presents in narrative form a critical review of the major trends of nineteenth century dream theory and investigations. Vande Kemp begins with a review of the oneirologically-directed literature produced between 1800 and 1860, then follows with a very detailed narrative of the work on dreams and dream theory conducted between 1860 and 1910. Specific sections are devoted to dreams and memory, reporting and recording dreams, consciousness in dreams, telepathy, death, dreams of prophecy, and the physical faculties employed in dreaming.

While one does not find the wealth of critical and interpretative data here in the style of the synthesis produced by Ellenberger, Vande Kemp makes up for this with the inclusion of a number of extensive passages written by these nineteenth century pioneers, and with the richness of her bibliographic and biographical data. There are included, for example, minute details not found elsewhere on the more obscure, though important, journals devoted to the dream during this entire century, not to mention biographical sketches of many noted and obscure toilers in the vineyards of dreamwork whose names, backgrounds, and reputations might otherwise be lost to history.

Unfortunately, this work lacks an index, and it requires the most determined scholar to pursue the wealth of information contained within these pages. But the rewards are worth the effort, for Dr. Vande Kemp has done a prodigious amount of work in musty libraries to produce what is a treasury of information on the idea and development of dream research in the pre-Freudian era.

**Van Dusen (Wilson). The Natural Depth in Man.** 197p. notes. Harper. N.Y., 1972.

One general, well written chapter on dreams in this memoir by a leading teacher of psychology, with some interesting sections on working with dreams, including Van Dusen's own dreams. The author is not a proponent of any school of dream analysis, but asks only that we view the dream for itself.

**Van Eeden (Frederik). The Bride of Dreams.** Translation by Mellie von Auw. 397p. M. Kennerley. N.Y., 1913.

Famous dream novel based on the noted psychologist's 500 dreams, recorded over a twenty-year span, ending in 1908. [Refer to Charles Tart in this bibliography for Van Eeden's "A Study of Dreams."] Van Eeden records flying dreams, soaring dreams, talks about the means of changing bodies in dreams, and coins terms embracing futuristic ideas of dreams, such as "joysphere," to suggest a sphere of joy which allows the dreamer to carry through with the pleasure of the dream during his next waking day. This kind of science fiction dream novel contains potential avenues for exploration which the author no doubt hoped would stimulate others to duplicate in some future world of scientific achievement.

**Van Lieshout (R.G.A.). Greeks on Dreams.** 280p. notes, biblio. H&S Publishers. Utrecht, Netherlands, 1980.

First printing of this (1971) Ph.D. thesis which the author completed at the University of Cambridge in England. The book deals primarily with the phenomenon of dreaming in the literature of pre-Classical and Classical Greece. The emphasis is historical and philosophical. Although E.R. Dodds served as an advisor on this project, no effort is made to expand on Dodds' pioneering cross-cultural researches.

Van Lieshout discusses the typology of early Greek dream experiences, the origin and mechanism of dreams, and the dream theories of Demokritos, Hippocrates, and Plato. There is a particularly valuable and extensive discussion relating to the various individuals, private and public, charged with dream interpretation during this era, as well as on early, little known dreambooks, and on the various oneirocritic methods commonly employed.

The author's work is scholarly and comprehensive, and deserves a place on the shelf of all interested in early dream theory and practice. Unfortunately, being primarily a scholar of classical Greek, Dr. Van Lieshout gives many seemingly promising passages only in classical Greek, which leaves this reviewer, and possibly many potential readers lacking proficiency in this language, with the disturbing notion that we are missing passages of great wisdom through our ignorance.

**Van Over (Raymond). Unfinished Man.** 210p. notes. biblio., index. World Publishing. N.Y., 1972.

Noted parapsychologist's book on the mind, discussing recent advances in psychical research, the role of hypnosis, a history of scientific research in parapsychology, the influence of psychedelic drugs, and studies in dreams. Mr. Van Over's chapters on dreams cover the usual ground of prophetic dreams, REM (dreaming sleep) experiments, and dream and sleep deprivation studies.

Unfinished Man is a well written, popular discussion of this topic from the occult perspective, but the author contributes nothing that I could find which advances evidence in support of the field of parapsychology. One wonders if proponents of this field do not need to re-examine their approach. Much material found in these books is a rehash of the contributions made by occult writers in the ninteenth and early twentieth centuries.

**Van Vogt (Alfred E.). The Search for Certainty.** About 200p. n.d. Copyright, 1970.

Essentially a copied manuscript held by the Library of Congress containing A.E. Van Vogt's radio talks, thoughts on women, and dream therapy. This famous science fiction writer's thoughts on patriarchial women and violent men are enough to hold anyone's attention, but the real reason for including this piece is the all too brief section on dream therapy, in which the author suggests one instruct himself or herself to dream in orderly fashion about individual traumatic incidents which psychotherapy could not resolve.

Van Vogt suggests that we have blocked out these dreams in later years, and that accidental or unconscious dreams of them will not resolve our conflicts so much as consciously working the dream through by a dream incubation process. He recommends using a timer as an alarm clock, set for every 90 minutes, then recording whatever dreams are recalled upon awakening.

**Varendonck (J.). The Psychology of Day-Dreams.** Introduction by Prof. Dr. S. Freud. 367p. notes, biblio., index. George Allen. London, 1921.

Varendonck, a Belgian psychologist, attempts to examine daydreams in light of recent Freudian theories of psychoanalysis, particularly considering a daydream in a context other than as "an abnormal psychic process," which was the accepted view up to that time. Yet Varendonck, while finding this mental phenomenon common to all men, does not conclude that it is a positive human process, but rather is one manifested by absentmindedness and distraction. "It causes errors and mistakes in our daily life . . . it is predominant in hysteria and neuroses . . . [and] it explains our behavior whenever our emotions prove stronger than our will."

Freud's two page introduction casts little further light on this topic, except to take issue with the author's central thesis. Freud asserts there is little difference between preconscious and conscious mental processes, so in daydreams one should focus on freely wandering thoughts rather than involve oneself in intentionally directed reflection.

**Vaschide (N.) & Piéron (H.). La Psychologie du rêve, au point de vue médical.** 96p. J.B. Bailliere et Fils. Paris, 1902.

An argument that the dream provides valuable data on the mental and physical condition of the dreamer, and might be employed advantageously as a diagnostic tool. The authors suggest that certain dreams indicate emotional and mental disturbances, while others may point to intestinal, cardiac, and pulmonary diseases as well as typhoid fever. Vaschide and Piéron provide case studies of the use of dreams in the diagnosis of insanity, neurosis (hysteria), and epilepsy. The authors were apparently not aware of Sigmund Freud's work.

**Vaughan (Frances). Awakening Intuition.** 228p. biblio., index. Anchor. Garden City, N.Y., 1979.

The author sees dreams as an aid in establishing a balance between the rational and intuitive functions. Vaughan reviews the recent literature in the area, suggesting that the reader make greater use of his or her dreams as in primitive societies. Too much emphasis has been placed, believes the author, on the use of dreams primarily in psychoanalysis and depth psychology. "Learning to understand your dreams is learning one of the languages of intuition. When you bring the light of consciousness into the dream world, intuition is validated, affirmed, and expanded."

**Vignoli (Tito). Myth and Science. An Essay.** 330p. index. D. Appleton & Co. N.Y., 1882.

A brilliant discourse on the relationship between dreams and myth, particularly in primitive and ancient cultures, developed more than thirty years before Carl Jung published his own dream theories. Dr. Vignoli, a peripatetic Italian scholar, believed that hallucinations of madness (apart from their morbid and organic conditions) derived from the same source which produces myths, dreams, and normal hallucinations. He appears to postulate a collective unconscious: "Since this innate faculty of myth is indigenous and common to all men, it will not only be the portion of all peoples, but each individual in every age, in every race, whatever may be their respective conditions."

The author devotes considerable attention to analogies, (his term for symbols) and traces these through a wide galaxy of primitive and ancient societies, suggesting their importance via the unconscious (though he did not use this word), to man today. "We have thus reduced the primitive origin of myth, of dreams, of all illusions, of normal and abnormal hallucinations, to one unique fact and genesis, to a fundamental principle; that is, to the primitive and innate entification of the phenomenon, to whatever sensation it may be referred . . . ."

The first Italian edition of this pioneering study, Mito e scienza, was published in Milan in 1879. The English edition appears to lack some of the scholarly annotations given in the original. An unfortunate shortcoming. Although this title is referred to in Freud's notes, he never cited the work in his published writings. Nor, as far as I can ascertain, did Carl Jung make mention of Dr. Vignoli's contribution. All the more regrettable, for Dr. Vignoli's effort represents an early masterpiece of inquiry into the relationship between man's origins, his myths, and his dreams.

**Villa Nova (Arnaldus de). Opera Omnia.** Basle, 1585.

Villa Nova, a Spanish doctor, philosopher, and alchemist, made the first serious attempt since Artemidorus to approach dream interpretation scientifically, supplying both a mystical and psychological explanation based on the dream theories of Aristotle. The author interpreted primarily by analogy as did Artemidorus, utilizing in his symbolism some astrological approaches as well. His late 13th century dreambook was important for conveying many Islamic and Middle Eastern concepts of dream interpretation northward into Europe. Villa Nova was reportedly the official dream interpreter to both the Kings of Aragon and Sicily.

**Vogel (Virgil J.). American Indian Medicine.** 584p. notes, biblio. index. University of Oklahoma Press. Norman, 1982.

Impressive, scholarly tour-de-force. While the emphasis is largely on botanical medicines, the author makes some particularly interesting observations on dreams. He notes, for example, that the early Iroquoian tribes believed that some disease was caused by unfulfilled desires revealed through dreams, and it was the task of the medicine man to probe his patient's dreams for the real cause of a disease.

Vogel writes that the Hurons considered a dream as an oracle that predicted future events, warned them of misfortunes, and also served as a physician for their sicknesses. The Hurons would obey their dreams before they would obey a leader. Quoting from a contemporary account, Jesuit Relations, the author notes that the dream in Huron society "prescribes their feasts, their dances, their songs, their games,--in a word, the dream does everything and is in truth the principal God of the Hurons."

Dreams play a role in Cherokee medicine similar to that of the Iroquois, with the medicine man as dream interpreter. The Cherokee belong to the same linguistic group as the Iroquois and Huron.

Interestingly, the early Cherokee and Iroquois Indians,

prior to and during the early period of contact with the white man, seemed to show very little tendency towards mental illness. Some writers believed this was due to their serene life and the absence of most tensions that plagued the white man. It also appears that the role of the medicine man in exploring the unfulfilled dreams and desires of the Indians, then setting a cure that "would follow the acting out of the dreams or the satisfaction of their desires," may have played a role in maintaining mental health.

**Vold (J. Mourly). Über den Traum.** 2 volumes. 870p. J.A. Barth. Leipzig, 1910-1912.

Certainly J. Mourly Vold is the legitimate precursor of all modern laboratory dream experimenters. Dr. Vold, a professor at the University of Christiania, conducted controlled dream experiments in a laboratory setting for almost twenty-five years prior to his death in 1907. His collected writings and notes were edited by Dr. O. Klemm shortly after his death.

His principal investigations centered on the use of cutaneous-muscular stimulation on the extremities (ankles and hands) of several hundred university students and teachers of both sexes. Vold then made a precise report on the relationship between stimulation and manifest dream content. Most of the first, and a large part of the second volume, contain the methodology and results of these experiments. Although reluctant to introduce dream interpretation into his research, the author could not refrain from comparing certain dreams with sexual fantasies, particularly flying dreams and those involving mounting steps. He based this conclusion largely on the intense feeling of bodily vibration accompanying such dreams as well as the frequency with which such dreams were accompanied by erections and emissions.

In a later edition of his book on the theory of dreams, Freud points to Vold's efforts as illustrative of the limitations of experimentally produced dreams. "I should recommend a study of this work," he wrote, "to anyone who wishes to convince himself of how little light is thrown on the content of individual dreams by the conditions of the experiments described in it and of how little help in general is afforded by such experiments towards an understanding of the problems of dreams." Freud would no doubt have modified this criticism in light of more recent experiments, particularly those postdating the REM discoveries.

**Volkelt (Johannes). Die Traum-Phantasie.** 208p. Meyer and Zeller. Stuttgart, 1875.

The Romantics viewed the dream as a means by which the soul freed itself from the body, whereas Volkelt argues that the dream is so interrelated to the body and bodily processes that the two cannot be separated. The dream mechanism, the "dream-phantasy," translates bodily or physical impressions into symbols. The body symbolized in dreams is perceived differently than is the physical body. Volkelt hypothesizes that the body image might be altered through attention to dreams.

He warns his colleagues that they pay far too much attention to the negative aspects, and should redirect their efforts to the study of positive fantasies, or symbols, inherent in dreams. He wrote, "The riddles of the universe, with the solution to which philosophers have often troubled themselves for naught, are solved by the dreamer nightly . . . . In fact, while dreaming, we are very near to the innermost of the universe; not with what we experience in the dream images, but with what we unconsciously are and do in the process of creating the dreams." Freud admits his indebtedness to Volkelt, quoting him nearly a dozen times.

**Von Franz (Marie-Louise). Alchemy. An Introduction to the Symbolism and the Psychology.** 280p. illus., index. Inner City Books. Toronto, 1980.

Noted Jungian scholar's attempt to explain alchemy as man's search for psychological balance and wholeness in himself. The rich body of symbolism includes much on their meaning in dreams.

**Von Franz (Marie-Louise). Passio Perpetuae.** 123p. notes. Damon Verlag. Zürich, 1982.

Examination of the life and dreams of this young martyr who perished in the Roman arena of Carthage in 203 A.D. Dr. von Franz places Perpetua's dream visions in the context of a world still in the process of transformation from the pagan to Christian era. She interprets these as a conflict between beliefs in two different and frequently conflicting God images, not unlike the struggle waged between good and evil.

**Von Franz (Marie-Louise). The Way of the Dream.** Windrose Films Ltd. Toronto, Canada, 1985.

Although not a book, I have included here an account of this ten-hour film. Dr. von Franz worked closely with Carl Jung for over thirty years, and reports that she has analyzed over 65,000 dreams. The film demonstrates her remarkable abilities in this area. Each sequence begins with a dream told by a particular dreamer. From her consulting room in Kusnacht, Switzerland, Dr. von Franz then proceeds with her on camera interpretation. There follows an interview with von Franz conducted by Fraser Boa, himself a Jungian analyst, in which she explains the reasons for her interpretations, and outlines her theory of dreams. The Way of the Dream allows the viewer to immerse himself in a dream, artfully retold by the dreamer, then follow the interpretation, through the words of the world's leading Jungian analyst.

**Von Franz (Marie-Louise). On Dreams and Death. A Jungian Interpretation.** Translation by E.X. Kennedy and V. Brooks. 193p. notes, bibliography, index. Shambhala. Boston and London, 1986.

Jungians believe the dreams of man depict stages in his own life development. The final stage is represented by dreams as preparation for, and in anticipation of, death. Carl Jung was particularly interested in this final stage of dreaming and of individuation, which he considered to be the culmination of man's life and being.

Marie-Louise von Franz expands on the ideas that Jung began but did not finish during his own lifetime. She explores what the unconscious has to tell us about impending death, and applies a Jungian interpretation to the death dreams and death experiences of men. Death comes to us through symbols and mythical images, argues the author, as does resurrection, the first ideas of which derive from Western alchemical tradition.

One of the most valuable chapters in this book treats Carl Jung's hypothesis that does not appear in any detailed sense in his books, but is obvious from a number of previously unpublished letters written late in his lifetime. Here Jung proposes that the physical and psychic energies of man fuse and ultimately change after death, and that this energy survives man's body. Personal accounts from individuals reported medically dead for many minutes are included to support Jung's arguments.

On Dreams and Death is a book filled with many fascinating speculations. Dr. Von Franz proposes that man's unconscious prepares him through his dreams not for death, but for transmutation, for a "continuation of the life process which, however, is unimaginable to everyday consciousness." She sees the symbols and mythical images of dreams as presenting "a thematic or structural harmony with the teachings of the various religions about life after death."

The author admits that she leaves many more questions unanswered than are resolved, and suggests too that her work here departs from the field of pure psychology and is better fitted, perhaps, to metaphysics. What the author does not claim, but seems equally obvious, is that Jungian psychology seeks a solution larger than those limited to medical therapeutic analysis and techniques. It seeks to establish a universal philosophy and religion designed to explain man's purpose in the universe.

All this will no doubt occasion a flurry of applause from dedicated Jungians, matched with equal amounts of skeptical critical response from those biological and experimental professionals working with dreams. This is to be expected for a theory that requires its adherents to adopt a commitment more of faith rather than of scientific proof in seeking goals identical to those of the world's great religions.

**Von Franz (Marie Louise, et al.). Im Umkreis des Todes.** 135p. notes, biblio. Daimon Verlag. Zürich, 1980.

Three Jungian papers by Marie-Louise von Franz, Liliane Frey-Rohn, and Aniela Jaffé on death. All three of these noted Jungian scholars describe the dreams of those approaching and entering death. The individual approaching death may have helpful dreams preparing him or her for entry into another form of existence. All the contributors see death, not as an end, but as a transformation.

At the conclusion of her paper, Dr. von Franz had a dream, about which she writes: "It seems to me that what I have tried to elucidate here are a few glimpses of an unknown country, separated from us while we are still living this life, as by fog, a country of which, however, one is, on occasion, given surprising views. The individuation process is preparation for death which is not an end, but a unique, rationally incomprehensible transformation."

**Waldhorn (Herbert F., reporter). The Place of the Dream in Clinical Psychoanalysis.** 106p. International Universities Press. N.Y., 1967.

Results of the Kris Study Group seminar of February 1965, consisting of 19 physicians of the New York Psychoanalytic Institute. One group supported the position of Dr. Leon L. Altman who suggested that the dream is to be used as any other form of communication from the patient, with the analyst recognizing how it differs in form from other communications. The dream is a product of mental functioning, being formed in an altered ego state (the ego function being particularly acute during dreaming) and the dream seems to have a special capacity to register recent experiences in a particularly sensitive way. A second group, with Dr. Waldhorn as spokesman, suggested that dreams have a special significance, and are of considerable value in conveying insights into the unconscious conflicts and processes in the patient's mental life. On the other hand, dream analysis, while having a place in techniques for gaining access to the unconscious, can no longer be considered "the sole or even the primary or preeminent technique at the disposal of the analyst." This group concluded, then, that "we analyze the patient, not the dream."

**Waller (John). A Treatise on the Incubus, or Night-Mare, Disturbed Sleep, Terrific Dreams, and Nocturnal Visions. With the Means of Removing These Distressing Complaints.** 115p. E. Cox & Son. London, 1816.

Dr. Waller, a Royal Navy physician, concentrates on the nightmare, "the disease that attacks always during sleep." He suggests nightmares are rarely fatal, although they might degenerate into epilepsy, a concern for those suffering from habitual rather than occasional nightmares. His descriptions of the physical symptoms and physiological changes during the nightmare are remarkably close to those described today.

Although Dr. Waller can only speculate on the physical and spiritual causes of the disease, he does suggest that the nightmare may originate "from no other cause than a defect in the digestive process." He writes that stomachs are frequently "distended with some acid gas, and I have often found the paroxysm of the nightmare to be the consequence of this distension alone . . . ."

Dr. Waller cites cases where "blood-letting" is recommended as a cure for the nightmare, but while admitting that such a therapy might prove advantageous under certain circumstances, it is likely that bleeding "would add fresh vigour to the monster, while it drains the vital powers of the struggling patient, and increases his danger."

The author suggests a change in diet, the possible use of carbonate of soda prior to sleep, moderate exercise, and temperance in food and drink.

**Walsh (William S.). The Psychology of Dreams.** 361p. notes, index. Dodd, Mead. N.Y., 1920.

A concise explanation of Freudian dream theory written by a practicing physician who suggests a practical approach to Freud. The author covers dreams as wishes, typical dreams, prophetic dreams, and the nightmare. There are interesting sections on the potential influence of the fears of the expectant mother on her child, but the author's explanation of the nature of the unconscious leaves something to be desired. Although published some twenty-onc years after Freud's The Interpretation of Dreams, the publisher still listed this title under the general subject: The Occult and Psychical Sciences. Largely dated today.

**Watkins (Mary). Waking Dreams.** Introduction by Stanley Krippner. 174p. notes, bibliography, index. Harper. N.Y., 1977.

Important book on the use of interior imagery and fantasy. Ms. Watkins traces the history of fantasy from its roots in Europe through its use in American psychotherapy. She expresses the necessity for a more active approach for getting in touch with the unconscious, rather than waiting for a nocturnal dream to occur. In addition, the nocturnal dream does not allow for direct dialogue between consciousness and the unconscious. Included are a number of practical exercises and techniques. A well written, basic source, with a solid bibliography.

**Watt (Henry J.). The Common Sense of Dreams.** 212p. biblio. Clark Univ. Press. Worcester, Mass., 1929.

Written because Dr. Watt felt that current psycho-analytic interpretations of dreams were unnecessarily obscure, even mystical, and that a simpler, more commonsense explanation was needed. Watt believed that in the vast majority of dreams the actual content of the dream has no inherent relation to the dreamer's sleep at all. He sees no conflict between the dream and present activity of the dreamer as a whole, but "since the act of sleeping or waking is one towards which our reluctance may at any time be directed as against any other act of ours, it is possible that some dreams may embody a solution of this reluctance."

The author cautions us that we have no reason to suppose that all dreams spring from acute conflicts. This may be the case with the clear-cut, vivid dreams we all recall, he says, but not with a majority of those which we find it difficult to recall. In interpretation, Dr. Watt believes that the dream gives its own emphasis. It is only necessary to use commonsense to look for it. He provides us with many examples of the dreams of Freud, Jung, Jones, and others, accompanied by their interpretations, then supplying his own.

**Webb (Wilse B.). Sleep. An Experimental Approach.** 250p. notes, biblio., index. Macmillan. N.Y., 1968.

"Critical Issues in Psychology Series," designed as a paperback source for undergraduate courses in psychology. Introductory level dream material interspersed, particularly as included in the supplementary readings.

**Webb (Wilse B.). Sleep. The Gentle Tyrant.** 180p. illus., index. Prentice-Hall. Englewood Cliffs, 1975.

Introduction to the physiology of sleep by a research professor of psychology at University of Florida. A nineteen page chapter on sleep and dreams supplies a brief overview of dream research, with emphasis on REM sleep.

**Webb (Wilse B.) & Agnew (H.W. Jr.). Sleep and Dreams.** 35p. in double columns. illus. Wm. C. Brown Co. Dubuque, Iowa, 1973.

The authors call this a "Self-Selection Textbook" designed for an introductory course on dreams at the college psychology level. Included are sections on variations of sleep, dream content, the function of dreams, and sections on sleep and hypnosis. At the end is a brief annotated bibliography.

**Weidhorn (Manfred). Dreams in Seventeenth-Century English Literature.** 167p. notes, biblio., index. Mouton. The Hague, 1970.

In this well-documented work, Weidhorn reports that this period did not produce any radical innovations in dream theory or the use of dreams in fiction. He sees in most writings a continuation of the old Platonic/ Stoic tradition of the dream's heuristic function, except perhaps for the writings of Hobbes, who approached their use with skepticism. Weidhorn writes that the philosophy of dreams remained bound to past traditions until the late 19th century Freudian revolution. In this respect he is incorrect, ignoring the substantial research and investigation conducted throughout the 19th century by German, French, and Italian investigators which Freud acknowledged as contributors to his own dream theories.

**Weilgart (W. John). Cosmic Dreams in Healing Words. Poems.** Oblong quarto. 18p. Cosmic Communication Company, Decorah, Iowa, 1971.

Dr. Weilgart, a Ph.D., and fellow of the Iowa Academy of Science, has produced an amazing number of monographs on linguistics, and has, as far as I can ascertain, developed a new language, UI, the "language of space," through which presumably one can "understand the Spirit's ethical relations."

If you follow this explanation so far, then you will delight in this monograph, which contains the dream poems of the Prophet, with glyphs, a phonetic transliteration, and accompanying translation into English.

**Weiman (Mark). A Bibliography of Books in English on Sleep, Dreams and Insomnia.** 130p. Moveable Foundation Workshop Press. Norwood, Penn., 1978.

A checklist rather than a bibliography, with neither abstract, annotation, nor topical index to guide the researcher. Although the section on dreams appears extensive, covering from pages 35 to 121, its value is questionable. Many of the titles are popular dreambooks, of little or no value. A number of other citations are rife with error.

In one case Mr. Weiman cites a book by Welsey, when he means Kelsey. He gives the printing date of another as 1875, when he means 1857. The Interpretation of Dreams is ascribed to A.A. Brill, when Mr. Weiman actually means authored by Sigmund Freud, and translated by A.A. Brill. Some titles are, in fact, nonexistent, as is Maurice Nicoll's The Rebirth Theme in Dreams. Other titles are totally incorrect. See particularly the title of the famous work by Brierre de Boismont.

I regret that I have the feeling reading this work that Mr. Weiman has listed many books on dreams, but read none of them. The bibliography is riddled with error and marked by indifferent editing. This is a source guide which will prove to be more disconcerting than helpful to the serious student of dreamwork. One saving grace, but an important one, is the number of citations included here of early English dream interpretation texts (sixteenth through the eighteenth centuries), more than one of which were previously unknown to this reviewer.

**Weisert (John Jacob). The Dream in Gerhart Hauptmann.** 120p. notes, biblio., index. King's Crown Press. N.Y., 1949.

Analysis of dreams and dream content in life and writings of Hauptmann based upon the dream theories of Freud and Jung. Particular attention is payed to the role of the dream in determining the course of this noted German dramatist's life and his works such as Der Grosse Traum [The Great Dream]. With an excellent bibliography of the role played by dreams and dreaming in German literature.

**Weiss (Harry B.). Oneirocritica Americana. The Story of American Dream Books.** 37p. plates. The New York Public Library. N.Y., 1944.

The most authoritative study published on American dream books dating from 1767. Mr. Weiss includes a listing of several hundred such titles, primarily popular fortune-telling and dream interpretation works designed for the unsophisticated. We find, for example, The Witch Doctor's Dream Book, of 1891, and Sibylline Oracles; or, Dreams and Their Interpretations; Being the Spanish Fate Book, of 1848. Mr. Weiss includes a brief history of American dream-book publishing, and some comparative statistical analyses of differing dreambook interpretations between 1804 and 1942.

**West (Katherine). Neptune's Plummet.** Amata Graphics. Lake Oswego, Oregon, 1977.

Reportedly with suggestions for individual work with dreams. Not seen.

**West (Katherine). Crystallizing Children's Dreams.** Amata Graphics. Lake Oswego, Oregon, 1978.

**Westerfield (Jonathan B.). The Scientific Dream Book and Dictionary of Dream Symbols.** 317p. Brewer, Warren & Putnam. N.Y., 1932.

Authored by two practicing psychologists who compiled this dictionary under the pseudonym, Jonathan B. Westerfield. Joseph Jastrow, in his review of this work, states that the authors cast "the older dream-lore where it belongs, in the rubbish heap of discarded ways of thinking . . . ." Instead, we find here a serious attempt at dream symbolization and interpretation, beginning with "abandoned" and ending with "zoo."

Although the dictionary does not provide the reader with a discussion of the different schools of thought on dream interpretation, most symbolic interpretation reveals a Freudian outlook, with emphasis on anticipation and wish fulfillment. The authors have written this work for the layman. The first 174 pages contain chapters on the nature and meaning of dreams, famous dreams, warning dreams, and sexual dreams. All this is pretty much dated today. The dream interpretations themselves are simple, lucid, and would prove helpful to the interested lay reader.

**Weygandt (W.). Entstehung der Träume.** Inaug. Diss. 196p. Leipzig, 1893.

Early attempt at experimentally producing dreams. The author, like Maury, was led to his studies by the effect of his own illness on the content of his dreams. Weygandt concluded that dream images result from sensory stimuli. He postulated that certain dreams might contain elements of wish fulfillment, though he did not utilize this term.

As a case in point, Weygandt devotes several pages to an examination of his thirst dreams. Weygandt argued that dreams do not free one from ordinary life, but lead directly back to the problems related to that life. Weygandt's work impressed Freud, who cited it extensively in his writings, and detailed Weygandt's thirst dream in a personal letter to Fliess in 1895.

**Wheelwright (Joseph B., editor). The Analytic Process: Aims, Analysis, Training.** [The Proceedings of the Fourth International Congress for Analytical Psychology.] 316p. biblios. Putnam's Sons. N.Y., 1971.

These twenty-one Jungian papers contain one, "The Transcendent Function of Dreams" by Dora Bernhard, which is of interest to us. Dr. Bernhard views the transcendent function "as a creative principle in the dealings of conscious with the contents of the unconscious." Dreams offering transcendence, she suggests, always point to a relationship problem. Dream analysis, in fact, is always relation-analysis. "A dream, even in a long dream story including exposition, crisis, and solution, merely reflects a present situation, the critical moment, from which only the transcendent function suggests an outlet." Dr. Bernhard provides dream case studies drawn from her own clinical practice, including mention of the dream-motif of twins and frequent number dreams.

**Whiteman (J.H.M.). The Mystical Life.** Introduction by H.H. Price. 250p. index. Faber & Faber. London, 1961.

An attempt to explain various forms of mystical experiences to the ordinary man and woman, written by a South African mathematician. In his all too brief discussion of the lucid dream, Whiteman draws a parallel between that form of dreaming and out-of-body experiences. Since one receives only a glimmer of this state while lucid dreaming, the author devotes the remainder of his book to an explanation of the state of "separation," and return in the processes of achieving out-of-body experiences. Regrettably, there is very little here for those interested in serious research on dreams.

**Wickes (Frances G.). The Inner World of Childhood. A Study in Analytical Psychology.** Introduction by Carl G. Jung. 342p. index. Appleton. N.Y., 1955.

A beautiful and sensitive book on child analysis, authored by a very special person with that rare gift for ready access to the "city of the child-soul." Through this fine writer, we are permitted to tread lovingly and understandingly past the high walls and through the thick gates protecting the psyche of the child.

Wickes approaches her study of the child from the Jungian point of view. This orientation is apparent in the two closing chapters of the book which deal with dreams and a correlation of dream and fantasy. She emphasizes the great role of fear in the child's life, both in waking and sleeping, and demonstrates how each child's dreams reflect clearly those fundamental problems of life which permit the sensitive analyst an opportunity for insight far beyond any other means of communication with a child's psyche. The author believes that her work with children's dreams supports Jung's theory of the collective unconscious. Each dream, she concludes, shows archetypal images handed down to us as our inherited wealth of inner life.

This delightful book was originally published in 1927. It was revised in 1955, and was re-issued in 1966. The Inner World of Childhood is a most worthwhile book, not only on dreams of children, but as a reminder of the role and importance of the tender and vulnerable psyche in all of our children.

**Wickes (Frances G.). The Inner World of Man.** 313p. 78 colored and black and white plates of psychological drawings and paintings. Farrar & Rinehart. N.Y., 1938.

In this later book Wickes seeks to examine the psyche of the adult as she did in her earlier work on the child. A major portion of the book is devoted to explaining man's ego, persona, shadow, animus, anima, and self through such unconscious communicative devices as the dream, drawings, and paintings.

The two lengthy chapters on dreams provide the analyst with a detailed case study of Jungian analysis and interpretation of dreams related in therapy sessions conducted over a long period of time. In the first, Dr. Wickes centers upon the image of the mother and the anima as they appeared in the first phase of analysis of a young man. In her second dream chapter, Dr. Wickes presents the dreams of a woman of late middle age. Analysis for the mature woman centered upon coming to grips with the animus figure in her dreams which was seen as the destructive factor in her life. Both chapters are recommended as classic examples of Jungian interpretation of dreams recalled during extended periods of therapy.

**Wickwar (J.W.). Dreams. What They Are and What They Mean. Being a New Treatment of an Old Subject.** 169p. George Sully & Co. N.Y., 1919.

A popular exposition of dreams and dreaming which went through at least three editions. Covers dreams through the ages, the cause of dreams, dream theories, prophetic dreams, and Freud's dream concepts. The author was a folklorist, and his chapter on old English customs which express themselves in the actions of people as well as in their dreams is the only one I found of interest, but even this centers more on folklore than on the dream. Dated.

**Wijsenbeek-Wijler (H.). Aristotle's Concept of Soul, Sleep and Dreams.** 259p. notes. Hakkert. Amsterdam, 1978.

Academic inquiry based on three of Aristotle's writings. Aristotle, always "rational," denied dreams have a divine origin, arguing that dreams could be either causes of actions or symptoms of bodily disturbances. Aristotle argued against divination by dreams, and confined his investigations to either biological or philosophical aspects of dreams and dreaming.

**Wilbur (George B.) & Muensterberger (Warner, editors). Psychoanalysis and Culture. Essays in Honor of Geza Roheim.** 462p. notes, bibliography. International Univ. Press. N.Y., 1951.

One paper in this collection is titled "Some Notes on Navaho Dreams" by Clyde Kluckhohn and William Morgan (pp. 120-131). The authors provide us with the dreams of five members of one Navaho family, which are viewed from an anthropological as well as depth psychology approach.

**Williams (Strephon K.). Jungian-Senoi Dreamwork Manual.** New revised expanded edition. 300p. illus. Journey Press. Berkeley, Calif., 1980.

Workbook used by Strephon Williams in both group and individual dreamwork sessions at the Jungian-Senoi Institute in Berkeley, California. Williams blends a number of successful techniques in teaching dream incubation, lucid dreaming, and self-help through dream understanding and psychic realization.

While one may not agree with all of Williams' theories and techniques, none can deny that he has been very successful, and that his work has been well received by the lay public with a personal interest in improving themselves via the dream. Williams has sold almost 20,000 copies of a manual that seems to offer something for everyone.

No less than thirty-five different techniques for working with dreams are described. The format is designed so as to give a step-by-step introduction to the basics of dreamwork. Yet one can easily become overwhelmed by the number of techniques introduced. This manual is probably best utilized in group dreamwork where one or two techniques can be worked with at any one time in a controlled setting.

I would suggest that the serious student of dreamwork consult this handbook to see if he or she can realize the results promised. I did find many of Strephon Williams' ideas and suggestions original and interesting.

**Williams (Strephon). Dreams and Relationship.** Journey Press. Berkeley, Calif., 1986.

Still in press as of this writing.

**Williams (Thomas R., editor). Psychological Anthropology.** 655p. notes, bibliographies, index. Mouton Publishers. The Hague, 1975.

This uneven collection of twenty-eight papers contains but one on dreams, a great disappointment to me in light of the significance of the study of dreams in cross-cultural research. The role of dreams in the evolution of religion and folklore is of some importance, and I am disheartened by the paucity of modern discussion and serious investigation in this area.

Vittorio Lantenari, the sole contributor to work with dreams, saves this collection for me. We find in his writing a stimulating exposition of the importance of dreams in the Nzema tribe of Ghana. His paper is based upon his collection of the dream accounts of Nzema religious leaders gathered during a field investigation in 1971.

Dr. Lantenari, an Italian psychoanalyst, centered his investigation on the cultural determinants of the dream--and the reverse of the same coin--the influence of the dream in determining culture.

From an analysis of dreams and the sociocultural role of those dreams, the author found that the acculturation process "has important roots in the activity of the unconscious." Indeed, as Lantenari points out, the contents of the dream and vision are the "initial expression" of the unconscious.

While he agrees that creative activity among peoples is a product of culture, Lantenari cautions that we not ignore the fact "that a considerable amount of this creative activity is deeply rooted in the irrational unconscious." The dream, the mechanism for revealing the unconscious, represents a stage halfway between rationality and irrationality, and the subjective and the objective. The individual employs conscious selection and interpretation of dream materials to "achieve social participation as interpreter and exponent of his own group." The group, on the other hand, "will find its frustrations, needs, and expectations symbolically expressed in the 'prophet's' dreams or in the ensuing myths and rituals."

The author supplies a number of dream examples to illustrate his point. Some of these dreams reflect a crisis within the Nzema tribe, giving rise to socio-religious movements. The Action Church, founded in 1948, was born as a result of a series of dreams given to Moses Armah, its spiritual leader. Mr. Armah's first three dreams are included, bringing to mind the three famous dreams of Descartes. Lantenari compares African prophetic dreams to the dream experiences of the Jamaican prophet Kapo, founder of an Afro-Christian movement, as well as to the dreams of a Puerto Rican Pentecostal leader in East Harlem, New York.

All this makes for engrossing fare in an investigative and analytical banquet of brilliance that deserves a better fate than being buried in this collection. All the more lamentable is the fact that Dr. Lantenari writes primarily in Italian, with all too little of his work available in English.

**Willoya (William) & Brown (Vinson). Warrior of the Rainbow: Strange and Prophetic Dreams of the Indian People.** 94p. Naturegraph. Happy Camp, Calif., 1962.

A passionate appeal for the brotherhood of man suggested by the great dreams and visions of a host of Indian wise men, including the Hopi, Huron, Blackfoot, and Sioux. Among the dozen dreams given, are those of contemporary Indians, including one by William Willoya, an Eskimo. The appendix contains an analysis showing the similarities between these dreams, followed by an explanation of the significance of Indian messianic dreams.

A common theme running through these Indian dreams centers on the dissolution of spiritual values during times of stress and turmoil, and the anticipation of a new Messiah who will unite mankind. This book casts a warm, delightfully positive light cast against today's darkness by a people with an intuitive wisdom that surpasses the sum total of technical knowledge produced by white man's civilization. Unfortunately, the world leaders who might profit most from this book are the least likely to open the cover. Written from the heart.

**Wilson (John). The Parsi Religion: As Contained in the Zandavasta, and Propounded and Defended by the Zoroastrians of India and Persia.** 610p. index. American Mission Press. Bombay, 1843.

Includes a translation of the Persian manuscript the Zartusht-Namah, composed by Zartusht-Behram in 1277 A.D. This work includes a biography of the prophet Zoroaster, although it was written some sixteen hundred years after Zoroaster lived. The author claims to have undertaken the biography as a result of a dream. He introduces many dreams throughout the text (pp. 477-522), accompanied by his interpretations. There appears to be no question that the dream played an important role in the ancient Parsi religion. The entire work is concerned with dreams, their interpretation, and a narration of the "miracles" produced by the prophet Zoroaster.

**Windsor (Joan & James C.). The Inner Eye.** 304p. index. Prentice Hall. Englewood Cliffs, N.J., 1985.

The authors write that dreams have proved to be the most effective means of communication between the self and other dimensions of the conscious being. They provide fifteen "rules of dream "interpretation" to enable the dreamer to "decode messages and unravel the mysteries that nightly flash onto the screens of our minds."

The Windsors believe that questions posed prior to sleep will be answered by one of several successive dreams that follow. They blend Jungian psychology with parapsychology, and concepts of Freudian wish fulfillment with Edgar Cayce's methods of dream interpretation. The Inner Eye casts an uncritical eye at essentially every major theory of dreams proposed in recent years, and mixes these together in a kind of dream cocktail that promises nothing less than total exhilaration for all those who will but drink from the cup.

**Winget (Carolyn) & Kramer (Milton). Dimensions of Dreams.** 414p. tables, biblio., index. University of Florida Press. Gainesville, 1979.

A major scholarly effort defining the essential methodological features of 132 dream content rating systems developed since the pioneering effort of Hall and Van de Castle of 1966. Winget and Kramer have captured the basic technical data required to select one from the many scoring devices available. A final section contains a thorough tabular summary of dream content studies. Dimensions of Dreams is a work of first-rate scholarship and is required reading for all with an interest in the quantification of dream content.

**Winnicott (D.W.). Playing and Reality.** 169p. biblio., index. Basic Books. N.Y., 1971.

First exposition in book form of Dr. Winnicott's theory of transitional objects and transitional phenomena. His theory proposes the existence of a transient phase in childhood between the periods of subjective infancy and objective perceptions. This previously unrecognized phase of childhood is characterized by fantasy and dreaming, during which critical data influencing the individual's later development may be locked in through the process the author calls "fixity of fantasying."

While the product of such fantasies may interfere with the individual's adjustment to the real or external world in later life, it may have even more damaging effects by interfering with "inner psychic reality, the living core of the individual personality." The continuance of this fantasy into adult life is most clearly evident in the individual's dream. The task of the analyst is to fashion from the bits and pieces of this "formlessness" a real meaning for the patient. The author draws dream examples from his own clinical experiences to illustrate his theories.

**Winson (Jonathan). Brain and Psyche. The Biology of the Unconscious.** 300p. glossary, notes, index. Anchor Press. Garden City, N.Y., 1985.

A very good history and survey of the idea of the unconscious and the role of modern science in attempting to investigate its nature and possible parameters. The book is particularly valuable in showing the historical developments following the 1953 Aserinsky and Kleitman discoveries. There is an excellent narrative of the step-by-step laboratory research, with each new discovery pointing the way to even more problems, and even more interesting discoveries.

While everyone should find the history of modern scientific investigations into the cause and nature of sleep and dreaming rewarding, I was less than enthralled with the author's description and evaluation of the psychological theories of the unconscious. Sigmund Freud, Alfred Adler, and Carl Jung come off very badly at the tip of Winson's pen. In my view, the author is especially weak in his reading of the origins and development of the theories of all three of these men. He presents a simplistic and occasionally inaccurate view regrettably all too common today among the behavioral scientists working with sleep and dreams in a laboratory environment.

Winson concludes, for example, that Jung's "fanciful ideas of archetypal figures" and the collective unconscious "can hardly be taken seriously today." He suggests that Freud, Adler, and Jung must have formulated their theories of the unconscious from materials found only in their own psyches. In some cases the author leads me to doubt that he has thoroughly read the writings of all three; in others, I question his interpretation of the materials he has read.

Possibly the best and most intriguing section of his book can be found in the chapter titled "Hypothesis," where Dr. Winson examines his theory of the biological basis of the unconscious. Here one finds the finest of analytical argument and writing, utilizing the most recent experimental evidence to develop a theory of the unconscious and of dreams that parallels closely David Foulkes' cognitive theory of dreams. If the concepts of Freud, Adler, and Jung are to be destroyed, it is men like Jonathan Winson and David Foulkes who will be wielding the swords.

In his analysis, the author develops his theory by relating new evidence to argue against the dream theories and interpretation given by Sigmund Freud. Winson begins with the postulation that the "task of associating recent events to past memories and evolving a neural substrate to guide future behavior is accomplished when the animal [including man] is asleep." The small prefrontal cortex processes new information during the day, then performs an integrative function during sleep, particularly REM sleep.

Winson argues that dreams are a "window on the neural process," that "set strategies" and modify human behavior. The author writes that we remember dreams only as a matter of chance, not as a need. Memory is not a function of the dream. He points to the fact that many people do not remember their dreams. Winson regularly introduces, then seeks to demolish, Freud's tenets. He sees Freud's idea of dream distortion, "not as a defense, but as a reflection of the normal associative process by which experience is interpreted and integrated." He refers to the idea that originated with Calvin Hall, that dream distortion is not a defense mechanism, "but an expressive means, and that dream symbols are chosen to represent a combined idea . . . ." Similarly, the author writes that Freud's idea of condensation in dreams could better be interpreted as "the natural bringing together of two or more entities that are closely associated with one another . . . " and that condensation does not function as a disguise, "but as a means of representing an unconscious idea."

To Winson, dreams tell us things as they are in the unconscious mind, but only as they are registered in the functional subsystem of the brain. What they tell us relates only to our unconscious personality, and "the statements, wishes, hopes, and fears of the unconscious personality." While the author writes that dreams frequently ignore "real problems of a most urgent nature . . . dreams may also recount conscious decisions, complete with the conscious reasoning by which they were made." In the final paragraphs of Dr. Winson's hypothesis, chemical and neurological explanations are given to explain forms of neurosis and psychosis.

Jonathan Winson and David Foulkes' theories of the dream are closely identified. [See Foulkes: Dreaming: A Cognitive-Psychological Analysis, in this bibliography.] I unconditionally recommend Brain and Psyche. It is a well thought out and stimulating, if exasperating, reading. It is important to remember that, while the author points to considerable experimental evidence to bolster individual points in his analysis of the dream, his "whole" picture of the cause, function, and use of the dream remains relegated to theory.

Still the sections on scientific research are first rate, and the resulting theory of both Winson and Foulkes cannot lightly be cast aside. Brain and Psyche will disturb traditionalists and warm the hearts of the behaviorists. There are more questions posed in this book than answered. But that has been the way of all investigations of the dream through the centuries.

**Winterstein (Hans). Schlaf und Traum.** 138p. Julius Springer. Berlin, 1932.

Early physiological studies on sleep and dreams by the director of the Institute of Physiological Studies at the University of Breslau. Dr. Winterstein's researches include preliminary investigations into the duration and frequency of dreams, dream content, and dream symbols. Included is one of the earliest scientific attempts to validate Freudian dream theory in the light of biological findings.

**Wiseman (Ann Sayre). Nightmare Help. A Parents' Guide.** 136p. illus. Ansayre Press. Cambridge, Mass., 1986.

One of the best primers available to parents searching for a method of dealing with their child's nightmares. Ann Wiseman, an artist, teacher, and therapist, has fashioned a book that will please and help adult and child alike. Each can turn to his or her own section in this fascinating work. The nightmares were "selected from the dreams of over two hundred school children between the ages of four and thirteen, as well as a few recurring adult dreams which started in childhood."

All the nightmares are real, recorded by the author as they were recounted by the child. So too are the drawings and sketches depicting each child's own night terror. Specific nightmares are presented in a personalized, almost storybook fashion. Just as the nightmare is considered the problem, so a solution follows. Each discussion is designed to explain the nightmare to both child and parent, and to dampen the fears of both. Parents will also find ample guidance for dealing with any future nightmares.

No theoretical or complicated discourse clogs this free-flowing guide. The author works entirely with the manifest content of the dream, on what she terms the literal level. Complex dream symbols are downplayed. Instead, she helps the child restage the problem presented in the dream, so that a better solution can be achieved. As Ann Wiseman writes, "Feelings get a chance to re-feel and re-act, as well as providing the dreamer with a way to feel safe enough to explore new solutions." This also allows feelings from the night's dreams to be integrated into the waking mind. The child or adult can then begin to master the problem which the nightmare presents. By drawing the dream, then changing even the smallest element, the dreamer exerts some control over his own life. Through "dialoguing" with the dream images, the child gains a sense of mastery and a feel for his own creative powers. Ann Wiseman includes numerous examples of the actual dialogues which took place as the children worked toward an acceptable solution. This technique has worked for the author during many years of dealing directly with both children and parents facing the problem of the child's nightmare.

No less impressive than Ann Wiseman's organizational and writing effort is the inclusion of sketches and drawings done by the children who actually experienced these nightmares. This collection of a child's imagery of fear is well worth the price of the book alone. Thc author calls her book, "For Children. From Children." How true. And what a delight it is.

**Witkin (Herman A.) & Lewis (Helen B., editors). Experimental Studies of Dreaming.** 242p. illus., notes, biblio., index. Random House. N.Y., 1967.

An informative survey of contemporary laboratory dream research in the 1960s, with a historical narrative by Frederick Snyder, an analysis of the psychological significance of the dream-sleep cycle by Charles Fisher, a review of recent studies on dream recall by D.R. Goodenough, and a study on presleep experiences and dreams by the two editors. There is also an excellent bibliography.

**Wolberg (Lewis R.) & Kardiner (A.). Hypnoanalysis.** 342p. index. Grune & Stratton. N.Y., 1945.

A major study on the practical application of hypnosis in psychotherapy, with a wealth of case study examples drawn from the authors' clinical practice. The authors begin with an explanation of their dynamic interpretation of hypnosis as an abbreviated form of therapy for patients unable to undergo prolonged treatment.

Hypnoanalysis, they argue, bypasses the principal limitation of the usual brief psychotherapeutic methods which must accept the deeper personality strata that foster a neurosis as a "liability" that cannot be altered. Hypnosis, on the other hand, brings out the transference phenomena rapidly and in a relatively pure state; it aids in the removal of resistance and in the absorption of interpretations.

Extensive use is made of hypnotic suggestion in "dream induction," a process of guided dream incubation. "Dreams are forms of ideational activity that may yield important clues to unconscious impulses, fears, and conflicts." The authors find both pattern and dream content are unique and important for the analysis. They trace the high degree of symbolization in dreams to the release of primitive types of representation, particularly of a phallic nature.

Drs. Wolberg and Kardiner argue that dreams, like conscious thinking, are dynamically motivated by urgent conscious and unconscious needs. By disclosing the repressed unconscious impulses and memories, dreams can yield important clues for the analyst. Both pre- and post-hypnotic suggestion are used to artificially stimulate the dream, which, the authors believe, is exactly the same as the spontaneous dream. While dreaming under hypnosis may bring about the recovery of forgotten memories or experiences, the patient is sometimes instructed to forget the dream upon awakening. That dream is then revealed under hypnosis, and in such cases the authors find that it should not be interpreted during the waking state. If the analyst feels the need to interpret a particular dream to the patient, he should do so only under hypnosis, cautioning the patient to accept or reject that interpretation in accordance with his own feelings as to its validity in his situation.

Interestingly, a large portion of this book centers

upon one clinical case, that of a schizophrenic male, and includes the use of pre- and post-hypnotic dream suggestion in his therapy. In the concluding section of the book, case studies using hypnotic dream suggestion are given.

**Wolf (Alexander) & Schwartz (Emanuel K.). Psychoanalysis in Groups.** 325p. biblio., index. Grune & Stratton. N.Y., 1962.

A presentation of the use of dreams in group therapy covers pages 135-161. One of the authors, Wolf, was a student of Karen Horney, who though not primarily interested in dreams, always asked Dr. Wolf about his patient's dreams. The authors suggest that in group therapy, the analyst is advised to monitor regularly the interrelationship between the patient reporting the dream and a co-patient, watching for aggression and related associations. A preliminary approach to the use of dreams in group analysis, which was obviously not the principal tool used by these authors in their practice.

**Wolff (Werner). The Dream: Mirror of Conscience. A History of Dream Interpretation from 2000 B.C. and a New Theory of Dream Synthesis.** 348p. illus., biblio., index. Greenwood Press. Westport, Conn., 1973.

Misleading title. The history of dream interpretation from the earliest times to the post-Freudian era is disposed of in some forty-odd pages. Certainly the more relevant portion of this book deals with the author's study of dream patterns as contrasted with dream elements, and his interpretation is based upon a synthesis rather than an analysis of the dream.

The interpreter first seeks to isolate the dream images (elements), then "synthesize" these into a meaningful whole.

Wolff believes that the dream gives clues to both past and present, serving as a guidepost towards the future. The dream synthesizes the thoughts, emotions, and aspirations, pointing toward the integration of the human psyche. The work contains a useful historical bibliography which unfortunately has not been revised since its original publication in 1953.

**Wolman (Benjamin B., editor). Handbook of Dreams. Research, Theories and Applications.** Consulting editors: Montague Ullman and Wilse B. Webb. 447p. notes, bibliographies, index. Van Nostrand Reinhold. N.Y., 1979.

This collection of fifteen papers is blessed with a few extremely good contributions. Others, in spite of the reputation of the authors, are a disappointment. One of the best is authored by the editor, Benjamin B. Wolman. Dr. Wolman should have abandoned the collective approach and written his own book. As far as I can ascertain, Wolman has never written his own book on this subject, and the world of dreams is the poorer for its absence.

The problems related to the interpretation of the dreams of schizophrenic patients is one of Wolman's special areas of interest. His observations, based on years of clinical practice, provide insights into a unique area of dream therapy. Wolman recommends caution in the interpretation of the dreams of schizophrenic patients. Many such dreams are obvious, picturing what is going on in the patient's mind, while others may be cries for help that the therapist dare not ignore. The author writes that even the suicidal impulses of schizophrenics can be identified at times through their dreams. Dreams may indicate as well the need for the therapist to alter his approach, even to modify therapeutic strategy. Wolman supplies several examples from his own experience. Particularly insightful is Wolman's observation that "Sometimes schizophrenics' dreams reveal uncanny telepathic experiences. On several occasions my patients have told me details on my life they could never have read or heard about."

Perhaps the most important contribution to this collection is Harry Fiss's seventy-five page paper reviewing and interpreting recent psychobiological research. Fiss has done an astounding amount of work that culminates with a brilliant synthesization of basic REM and NONREM research into sleep and dreams conducted by experimental scientists between 1953 and 1979. The author presents an informative discussion of restorative vs. adaptive theories of sleep (Hartmann and Dement vs. W.B. Webb), confessing later that he leans toward Webb's adaptive theory of both sleep and dreams.

An overview of major research findings is followed by Fiss's proposals treating the major benefits realized to date. He ranks the evolution of the dream laboratory as a major advance in the development of scientific method and experimentation. The identification of the two main states of dreaming (REM and NONREM), the determination of the five stages of dreaming, and the discovery of the cyclical process of the dream are noteworthy achievements. So also are additions to our knowledge relating to the psychological and biological functions of sleep, findings relating to the area of dream recall and memory, and more sophisticated distinctions between the nightmare and night terror.

From his review of the research data, Fiss concludes

that the dream serves not one but multiple functions. He suggests that Freud would have expanded his concept of wish fulfillment in favor of a broader definition of the purpose of the dream had he been aware of modern research evidence. While he applauds the gains realized in the fields related to the biology of dreaming, Fiss maintains that many important answers to the dream await rigorous experimental effort directed towards the psychology of dreaming.

Important links between dreams and the physiological events of sleep are established in the paper given by Robert W. McCarley and J. Allan Hobson. The authors note that specific kinds of information relating to the commands given the eyes to move may play an important role in dream construction. Furthermore, shifts in the visual world of the dream may reflect a synthesis of information about eye movements, just as bodily movement during sleep may also play an important role in dream construction. McCarley and Hobson also argue that shifts and plot changes in dreams may be related to the temporal course of activation of the transverse nerve on the ventral surface of the brain. An "activation-synthesis hypothesis of dream generation" is proposed in which the same mechanisms apply to both dream and waking, conscious activities. These combine sensory, motor, and bodily information systems. "Dreams are not a result of an attempt to disguise but are a direct expression of this synthetic effort," conclude the authors.

Papers on extrasensory communication through dreams by Jon Tolaas and Montague Ullman, and on controlling dreams and dream content by Charles Tart are largely restatements of what these authors have said in earlier writings. Both point to the paucity of research that has been undertaken in more recent years. Tolaas and Ullman write that what is new only serves to "buttress the evidence from other sources for the occurrence of extrasensory effects in dreams," while Tart writes that what is new only affirms his previous conclusions. Tart did find posthypnotic suggestion to be the most powerful technique for content control when used in a presleep phase, while lucid dreaming may be the most powerful form of content control during the dream proper, although he admits there exists little scientific proof to back this latter contention.

Research on drugs, REM sleep, and dreams by Thomas Roth, Milton Kramer, and Patricia J. Salis, and a paper on dreams in psychopathology, this time by Kramer and Roth alone, serve up only double-header disappointments. The two papers observe that no conclusions are possible since research in both areas is either insufficient or nonexistent. These notations may have a place in a technical journal, suggesting areas for further research, but hardly in a handbook on dreams. What is presented in over thirty pages of text could easily have been condensed into a few paragraphs.

Some of the papers in Handbook of Dreams represent a preliminary writing of what the author has later developed into a book. Richard M. Jones, in his paper on dreams and education, supplies ideas and examples more expertly presented in his subsequent book, The Dream Poet. Much of David Foulkes' paper serves as a brief introduction to a topic better covered in his Children's Dreams, published in 1982. Foulkes can never be totally ignored, however, since fresh and disturbing ideas populate all his writings. In this early statement of his cognitive theory of dreams, Foulkes argues that children's dreams are competently executed through sequences demonstrating considerable cognitive skill and, contrary to the general view, children's dreams are not especially frightening.

Most disappointing were the papers reviewing traditional psychotherapeutic dream interpretation. Thayer A. Greene's paper on Carl Jung's theories, and that of Susan Knapp on the phenomenological theory of dreams developed by Karen Horney, Harold Kelman, and David Shainberg are well written. But both authors seem to be writing in a vacuum, ignoring entirely what I believe should have been the aim of this collection: a matching of traditional dream interpretation theories with recent experimental evidence. I find no arguments for or against REM experiments here, in spite of the fact that many behaviorists point to REM and biological research as adequate evidence in refutation of standard psychotherapeutic dream theory. Indeed, the authors seem to operate as if Aserinsky, Kleitman, and their successors had never existed.

This same criticism applies to Leo Gold's paper on Alfred Adler's holistic approach to dream interpretation and, to a lesser extent, to Richard M. Jones' analysis of Freudian and post-Freudian theories of dreams. An ending discussion of Montague Ullman's adaptive theory of dreams and Erik Erikson's epigenetic theory of individual human development saves Jones' paper, even if only in the final pages. Jones suggests that Erickson's epigenetic theory was developed to complement Freud's theory of neurotic development and, in fact, supports Freud in its essential aspects. The author concludes that modern post-Freudian psychiatric dream theories are not at war with Freud. He does not deal with the potentially more damaging experimental challenge, however.

Montague Ullman's paper on the experiential dream group, and Wilse B. Webb's historical perspective of dreams in Western thought, promise much but regrettably deliver less. Webb undertakes an impossible task of condensing the entire history of the idea of the dream into nineteen pages. Webb ends serving up a tantalizing appetizer while leaving no space for the meal. Ullman, who certainly has both the ability and the talent, throws off a light, ephemeral sketch on the experiential dream group that lacks the substance one expects in a handbook analysis of this topic. Montague Ullman has done excellent work on dreams, and has produced some first-rate writing. Unfortunately this paper does not rank in that category.

Even the splendid efforts of Wolman, Fiss, McCarley and Hobson fail to turn the Handbook of Dreams into a true handbook of dreams. All the contributors to this collection have excellent credentials. All the more reason for disappointment.

**Wolstenholme (G.E.W.) & O'Connor (Maeve, editors). CIBA Foundation Symposium on the Nature of Sleep.** 416p. notes, illus., index. Little Brown. Boston, 1961.

Scholarly work emphasizing neurological and physiological studies. One chapter on the nature of dreaming is authored by Nathaniel Kleitman stressing only those factors which lend themselves to quantitative measurement.

**Wood (Clement). Dreams: Their Meaning and Practical Application.** 282p. Greenberg Pub. Sykesville, Md., 1931.

A popular, readable book on dream interpretation. After a varied career as lawyer, judge, and teacher, Clement Wood turned to psychology and writing. Wood contributed many articles on dreams to his syndicated newspaper column, and this book contains the best of his writings on this subject. Unfortunately, many of Wood's interpretations seem oversimplified, particularly with the knowledge we have today. The author also makes suggestions to his readers regarding self-interpretation of dreams that are equally simplistic. Reprinted in 1941 under a new title, Your Dreams and What They Mean.

**Woodman (Marion). The Owl Was a Baker's Daughter. Obesity, Anorexia Nervosa and the Repressed Feminine.** 139p. illus. Inner City Books. Toronto, 1980.

This Jungian analyst uses dreams among other techniques to explore "the personal and cultural loss of the feminine principle." This loss can be detected in both obesity and anorexia. Dream examples of anorexics and obese women reflect how the outer body mirrors the inner psyche.

**Woodman (Marion). Addiction to Perfection. The Still Unravished Bride. A Psychological Study.** 204p. biblio., index. Inner City Books. Toronto, 1982.

Study of the psychology and attitudes of the modern woman, faced with cultural one-sidedness that favors male father-image values. Dr. Woodman describes the clinical workshop designed to integrate the female body and psyche, "to take the healing symbols from dreams, put them into the unconscious body areas and allow their energy to accomplish the healing work." Dream symbols rather than images are emphasized so that the subject would not become fascinated with dream interpretation.

Dr. Woodman believes that her clinical practice demonstrates that a "body workshop" is as necessary in analysis as dream work. "Body movements, I realized, can be understood as a waking dream. In its spontaneous movements the body is like an infant crying out to be heard, understood, responded to, much as a dream is sending out signals from the unconscious."

**Woodman (Marion). The Pregnant Virgin. A Process of Psychological Transformation.** 204p. notes, illus., index. Inner City Books. Toronto, 1985.

In this discussion and celebration of the female psyche, Dr. Woodman introduces a host of archetypal dream symbols, and discusses utilizing the dream and active imagination in integrating an awareness of the physical body with the whole self. She includes numerous dreams in this Jungian-oriented exploration of the inner virgin, the woman "one-in-herself" who is ever-expanding her potential in life.

**Woods (Ralph L., editor). The World of Dreams.** 389p. Random House. N.Y., 1947.

Invaluable anthology containing writings on dreams and dream theory from early Egypt through Freud to Jung. Woods examined over 2,500 medical and nonmedical volumes before he made his final selections "of the world's most interesting and significant writings on dreams." He then added a biographical note to each selection. A scholarly work, yet also of interest to the layman. To some degree superseded by the next title.

**Woods (Ralph L.) & Greenhouse (Herbert B., editors). The New World of Dreams.** 439p. biblio. index. Macmillan. N.Y., 1974.

A streamlining of Woods' original anthology which serves the original collection very badly indeed. Nearly

150 of the original selections, not to mention all biographical data, have been omitted. While eighty new selections have been added, including some reflecting new REM research, the end result is less than totally satisfying.

The new editor has failed to provide a commentary linking one section to the other, substituting a series of glib summaries which do nothing for the book. Disappointing edition, though still useful for the beginner.

**Wortis (Joseph). Fragments of an Analysis with Freud. A First-Hand Account.** 208p. facs., index. Simon & Schuster. N.Y., 1954.

Day-by-day diary of one of the last persons to undergo personal psychoanalysis with Freud. The analysis took place over a four month period in 1934, when Freud was 78 years old. Numerous references to the writer's dreams are given, with Freud's comments and interpretations reported. Reprinted in 1984.

**Wundt (Wilhelm). Outlines of Psychology.** Translated by Charles Hubbard Judd. Third Revised English Edition. 392p. notes, index. Wm. Engelmann. London/N.Y., 1907.

Wundt viewed the dream as a product derived from bodily sensations, classing them into two groups, those due to "nervous stimulation" and those due to "association." Sleep, dreams, and hypnosis, he wrote, are "essentially the same in their psychophysical conditions." All are essentially physiological in nature. Wundt found that the movements of the body, such as breathing, extension of the limbs, and so forth, could give rise to differing dream fantasies. Similarly, the limbs placed in an awkward or uncomfortable position might excite different dream images.

Dr. Wundt founded the first laboratory in experimental psychology (1879), and his writings exerted an influence on both Freud and Jung. Freud argued that his theory of the "wish to sleep" filled in the gap between the dream theories of L. Strumpell and W. Wundt.

**Yolen (Jane). Dream Weaver.** Illus. by Michael Hague. 80p. colored illus. William Collins Pub. N.Y., 1979.

Fairy tales in a dream setting for children. For a penny a dream, the old blind Dream Weaver weaves dreams for seven sets of passers-by. Wonderfully written book which could be utilized in a young adult's dreamwork class.

**Zeller (Max). The Dream. The Vision of the Night.** 183p. Analytical Psychology Club of Los Angeles. Calif., 1975.

Collected papers of leading West Coast Jungian analyst, edited by Janet Dallett. Several studies relate to dreams, including "The Poltergeist Phenomenon in a Dream," and "The Dream, the Vision of the Night," a lecture on fantasy, dreams, and myths.

**Zen (Giovanni). I Sogni de San Francesco D'Assisi. Studio critico-pschologico dei due sogni della conversione.** 194p. notes, biblio. Pontificio Ateneo Antonianum. Rome, 1975.

Historical and psychological analysis of the two dreams of conversion of St. Francis of Assisi, during which, following a visitation by God, St. Francis believed he was called upon to spread the word of poverty as the path to Heaven. Dr. Zen examines this dream from the Aristotelian, Augustinian, Cartesian, Freudian, Jungian, and cross-cultural points of view. He concludes that St. Francis' dream experiences were rich in both symbolism and allegory. Both ancient and modern theories of dream interpretation, he continues, do not refute either the interpretation or significance of these dreams.

The principal effort in this work consists of comparing the various historical versions of each of St. Francis' dreams, and all too little effort is devoted to an examination of these dreams in light of the concepts of the modern schools of psychotherapy. Both Freud and Jung, for example, are dealt with in less than six pages. Dr. Zen submitted this thesis to the Papal Pontificial College.

Like Descartes, St. Francis serves as a prime example of the individual who dedicates his life to the revelations resulting from his dreams. Both pursued their message with unswerving and unquestioned dedication.

**Zinker (Joseph). Creative Process in Gestalt Therapy.** 278p. illus., biblio., index. Brunner/Mazel. N.Y., 1971.

In one section the author reviews how a dream is reported by one group therapy member, worked out at the individual level, then developed into a group experiment. In this way, Zinker states, "Each individual may reap fruit from the original imagery of the dreamer." Brief but important portions of this book are concerned with the dream as a creative process.

**Zlotowicz (Michael). Les cauchemars de l'enfant.** 350p. notes, biblio., index. Presses Universitaires de France. Paris, 1978.

An extensive collection of research into the function of the nightmare in early childhood, authored by a psychologist at the Laboratoire de Psycho-Biologie de l'Enfant. The basic body of material consists of 500 manifest dream records of both male and female children from five to ten years of age. The approach is Freudian, detailing the role of aggression and frustration, wish fulfillment, and guilt in the children's dreams. Individual sections are devoted to symbolism, and Freudian theory and application. An extensive appendix contains the manifest content and interpretation of the nightmares documented in the book.

**Zolar's Encyclopedia & Dictionary of Dreams.** 417p. Arco Publishing Company. N.Y., 1984.

The most widely published popular dream dictionary in the United States, and an ideal example of why dream chapbooks remain popular century in and century out. Zolar's work appears in England under the title, The Interpretation of Dreams. Zolar, who apparently does not claim a first name, began his writing and advice-giving in 1932, and the publisher Arco has been issuing tens of thousands of Zolar's books on the occult for many years.

Zolar, to be sure, has no truck with Sigmund Freud. His dictionary is unencumbered with phallic symbols. Look not for pole or staff, for they are not included in a dictionary where even the serpent is interpreted in fourteen different ways, none of which refers to sex. I read a brief review of Zolar where the writer suggested that, midst Zolar's bald assertions about the meaning of dream images, still his dictionary was "often resonant with archetypal meanings." Certainly the very mass of Zolar's verbiage will give even the most demanding of Jungians enough archetypes to fill a thousand collective and unconscious psyches.

I don't recommend that the reader look too deeply into Zolar for the classic archetype, however. Instead read Zolar for fun, and as a popular psychologist almost without peer, who knows what the public wants to know about their dreams, and gives it to them.

**Zosimos of Panopolis. On the Letter Omega.** Edited and Translated by Howard M. Jackson. 64p. notes. Scholars Press. Missoula, Montana, 1978.

Zosimos was a third century alchemist and resident of Alexandria, Egypt. He is believed to have been born in Greece. Zosimos developed a theory of alchemy rich in imagery.

On the Letter Omega provides some insight into the mystic, alchemical imagery of Zosimos, whose writings suggest that many alchemists' quest for the philosopher's stone was not unlike modern man's search for his inner self. Zosimos is also remembered for his dream visions which appear to have played a significant role in the development of his alchemical theories. Carl Jung (Collected Works, vol. 13, Alchemical Studies, pp. 59-65), has translated important portions of these from the classical Greek.

# Indices

# Name Index

# Subject Index